WHAT WOULD LINCOLN DO?

*Lincoln's Most Inspired
Solutions to Challenging Problems
and Difficult Situations*

WHAT WOULD LINCOLN DO?

*Lincoln's Most Inspired
Solutions to Challenging Problems
and Difficult Situations*

D AVID A C ORD

SOURCEBOOKS, INC.®
NAPERVILLE, ILLINOIS

Published by Sourcebooks, Inc.
P.O. Box 4410, Naperville, Illinois 60567-4410
(630) 961-3900
Fax: (630) 961-2168
www.sourcebooks.com

Library of Congress Cataloging-in-Publication Data
Acord, David.
  What would Lincoln do? : Lincoln's most inspired solutions to challenging problems and difficult situations / David Acord.
      p. cm.
  Includes index.
  1. Lincoln, Abraham, 1809-1865--Political and social views. 2. Lincoln, Abraham, 1809-1865--Philosophy. 3. Lincoln, Abraham, 1809-1865--Oratory. 4. Lincoln, Abraham, 1809-1865--Correspondence. 5. Illinois--Politics and government--To 1865--Decision making. 6. United States--Politics and government--1861-1865--Decision making. 7. Communication--Handbooks, manuals, etc. 8. Leadership--Handbooks, manuals, etc. 9. Professional ethics--Handbooks, manuals, etc. 10. English language--Handbooks, manuals, etc. I. Lincoln, Abraham, 1809-1865. II. Title.
  E457.2.A425 2009
  973.7092--dc22

                               2008037591

Printed and bound in the United States of America.
BG 10 9 8 7 6 5 4 3 2 1

Contents

Note to the reader: Many of Abraham Lincoln's letters are reprinted in this book. In some instances, paragraph breaks have been added to make reading the letters easier. Any edits to the letters are noted with brackets or ellipsis.

Introduction

ABRAHAM LINCOLN WASN'T HANDSOME. THE sixteenth president of the United States didn't have a smooth, silky voice or a magnetic personality that instantly drew crowds to him. In fact, he had few of the qualities we expect in modern politicians. Whiter-than-white teeth? Sorry. A stable family life, including a happy wife? Negative. Historians have often noted that had Lincoln lived in modern times, he would have had trouble getting elected to a seat on his local city council, much less the highest office in the land.

Nevertheless, he became one of the most successful politicians in American history—although using "politician" to describe Lincoln is like using "basketball player" to describe Michael Jordan. Lincoln transcended politics, and his era, by holding the country together in the midst of a savage civil war and eventually ending the scourge of slavery. When an assassin's bullet cut his life short in 1865, he had already become an inspiration to millions around the world, one of the few leaders whose name is synonymous with freedom.

And therein lies the problem. For generations, Lincoln has been a mythic, larger-than-life presence whose image adorns our currency and whose monument towers over Washington D.C. The sheer enormity of his legend tends to overshadow both the true nature of his accomplishments as well as what was, in many respects, a profoundly normal life. It's easy to forget that Lincoln was a flesh-and-blood man who faced the same challenges in the nineteenth century as many of us face today. He didn't come from a rich family; in fact, he was born into poverty and his parents had little education. In an autobiographical sketch he wrote in 1860, he noted that his father, Thomas, "grew up litterally (sic) without education. He never did more in the way of writing than to bunglingly sign his own name."

Lincoln never attended school regularly and was largely self-educated, borrowing books whenever he could to learn the rudiments of writing and rhetoric. In that same autobiographical sketch, while writing about himself in the third person, he said that "the aggregate of all his schooling did not amount to one year. He was never in a college or Academy as a student; and never inside of a college or academy building till since he had a law-license. What he has in the way of education, he has picked up. After he was twenty-three, and had separated from his father, he studied English grammar, imperfectly of course, but so as to speak and write as well as he now does. He studied and nearly mastered the Six-books of Euclid, since he was a member of Congress. He regrets his want of education, and does what he can to supply the want."

As he grew into adulthood, Lincoln struggled with depression and was constantly under stress, both financial and political. Before he entered politics, his career had more ups and downs than a roller coaster. He worked as a boatman on the Ohio River, a farm-hand for various neighbors, a postmaster, a surveyor, and even a clerk at a general store. When he was just twenty-three, he opened his own general store with a partner, William Berry, but the venture failed, and he was left deeply in debt.

But that was just the beginning. As his political career progressed, he faced fierce battles in the workplace: rival politicians—and sometimes even his own subordinates—clashed with him over his ideas and management decisions. Vicious rumors about him were routinely spread. In his personal life, Lincoln had to deal with troublesome relatives and close friends who relied heavily on him for emotional support during personal crises. He worked long hours and was extremely ambitious, but struggled to balance his professional goals with his roles as friend, husband, and father.

And yet, somehow, he pulled it off. Lincoln triumphed, and inspired a loyalty among his friends and colleagues so intense that we still marvel over it today.

How?

You could fill a small library with books that attempt to answer that question by analyzing his political philosophy, religious beliefs, and psychological make-up. This is not one of those books. The truth is, it takes many things to make a man great and, after all is said and done and his numerous character traits and flaws have been endlessly analyzed and categorized, we may still never be able to identify one special X factor that separates the legends from the rest of us.

But there is one often overlooked trait of Lincoln's that deserves serious examination—not for what it tells us about *him*, or because it provides the "big answer," but for how it can help *us* live better lives and succeed personally as well as professionally.

In addition to being a thoughtful and decisive leader, the sixteenth president of the United States was, first and foremost, a master *communicator*. If you want to understand how Lincoln became such a respected figure in politics, and why so many people put their trust in him, look no further than his letters. There you will see a man fully in control of not only the English language, but of his emotions. Somehow, during those long hours spent poring over borrowed books—from a biography of George Washington to works on English grammar, the plays of Shakespeare, and classics like *The Pilgrim's Progress* and *Robinson Crusoe*—Lincoln cracked the code. He realized that if he intended to succeed in the rough-and-tumble world of American politics, he would have to put just as much care into the expression of his core beliefs as he had into creating them in the first place.

And that's exactly what he did. Much of Lincoln's success can be attributed to the way he communicated his thoughts and ideas on the written page and the public stage. The qualities of an excellent writer—clarity, conciseness, the ability to explain complex thoughts in easy-to-understand language, and the wisdom to avoid emotional, *ad hominem* attacks on one's opponents—are present in almost every line of his speeches and prolific correspondence. Even a casual reader flipping through his collected writings quickly realizes that Lincoln took as much care in responding to a letter from a casual friend as he did when communicating with generals on Civil War battlefields.

Yet, aside from a handful of memorable speeches and quotations, Lincoln's written legacy has mostly been forgotten. This book is an attempt to shed light on Lincoln's written mastery and remind people that there was much more to the man than the Civil War and the Gettysburg Address. All presidents leave behind a paper trail to some extent, but Lincoln's collected works rivals Thomas Jefferson's for the insights they give into his inner life.

But, first and foremost, this book is meant to be a practical manual for anyone who wants to become a better writer or communicator, whether you're composing an email, speaking in front of five hundred people or talking on the phone to your best friend. By quickly studying just a few key excerpts from Lincoln's masterful letters and speeches, you can avoid common mistakes and learn how to:

- Calmly discuss highly emotional issues without losing your temper
- Assemble your thoughts and express yourself in a straightforward, logical manner
- Say or write what you really feel without unintentionally hurting someone's feelings
- Stay on point and avoid getting distracted by other arguments
- Explain your point of view calmly and quickly— say in twenty-five words what it takes most people a hundred or more to express
- Avoid writing long, rambling emails or

presentations and simply, quickly get to the heart of the matter

- Give advice to a friend or relative without being overbearing

The lessons in this book can be applied to almost any situation. Regardless of whether you're writing a business email to a colleague who refuses to cooperate on an important project, trying to persuade a huge client to go along with your marketing plan, or penning a letter to a best friend or spouse about a deeply personal issue, Abraham Lincoln's writings, though more than a century old, provide the blueprint you need.

Part I:

The Personal

Sphere

CHAPTER 1

Responding to Rumors

H OW DO YOU RESPOND TO SOMEONE WHO threatens to spread damaging information about you? Lincoln faced that dilemma in 1836 when he was just twenty-seven years old and running for reelection to his seat in the Illinois state legislature. Colonel Robert Allen, a political opponent, began telling voters that he had dirt on Lincoln, but that out of the goodness of Allen's heart, he'd decided not to tell anyone. It was a particularly devilish way to trash the reputation of the future president. Allen was saying, in effect, that Lincoln had done something wrong (either legally or morally), but Allen was too dignified to reveal the scandalous details.

Instead of getting upset and letting his emotions get out of hand—which most of us would probably do in the same situation—Lincoln responded with class, brevity and, most of all, strength.

LETTER TO COLONEL ROBERT ALLEN
(JUNE 21, 1836)

Dear Colonel,

I am told that during my absence last week you passed through this place, and stated publicly that you were in possession of a fact or facts which, if known to the public, would entirely destroy the prospects of N.W. Edwards and myself at the ensuing election; but that, through favour to us, you should forbear to divulge them.

No one has needed favours more than I, and, generally, few have been less unwilling to accept them; but in this case favour to me would be injustice to the public, and therefore I must beg your pardon for declining it. That I once had the confidence of the people of Sangamon, is sufficiently evident; and if I have since done anything, either by design or misadventure, which if known would subject me to a forfeiture of that confidence, he that knows of that thing, and conceals it, is a traitor to his country's interest.

I find myself wholly unable to form any conjecture of what fact or facts, real or supposed, you spoke; but my opinion of your veracity will not permit me for a moment to doubt that you at least believed what you said. I am flattered with the personal regard you manifested for me; but I do hope that, on more mature reflection, you will view the public interest as a paramount consideration, and therefore determine to let the worst come. I here assure you that the candid statement of facts on your part, however low it may sink me, shall never break the tie of personal friendship between us.

I wish an answer to this, and you are at liberty to publish both, if you choose.

In technical terms—and I don't mean to confuse anyone here by using dense, complicated language—this is known as calling someone's bluff. Lincoln is saying, in effect: *Come and get me, Allen. You want to throw dirt? Throw it. You're not going to scare me.*

Let's examine why this short letter is so effective, and the lessons it can teach us about how to respond effectively—even elegantly—to threats and hostile behavior in general.

1. **Lincoln didn't lose his cool.** He didn't resort to name-calling or impugning Allen's character, which he had every right to do; after all, here was a man who was trying to ruin not only Lincoln's reputation, but his political career as well. But Lincoln was shrewd. Regardless of whether Allen actually had damaging information about him, he knew that if he responded in an emotionally overwrought manner, he would be playing right into his enemy's hands. Even if Lincoln was completely innocent of any bad behavior, Allen could take a letter filled with venom and anger and use it against Lincoln, either as proof that he had something to hide ("Why get so upset if you're innocent?") or that he didn't have the temperament for an important elected office ("If he flies off the handle at me, what will he do when he's faced with even bigger problems?").

   No, Lincoln chose a wise path: don't give your enemies any ammunition. If a fool threatens you, make sure your reaction to the threat doesn't turn you into a fool as well.

2. **Lincoln took the high road.** Lincoln betrayed not one iota of anger or frustration at Allen's actions. Instead, he turned the tables on Allen by encouraging him to disclose the damaging information for the good of the people of Illinois. He took himself out of the equation altogether; it was no longer a Lincoln-Allen feud. He told his enemy, in so many words: *Look, the people deserve to know what kind of man they're electing to the legislature. If you know something, tell them—it's your duty as an American.* Allen might have been expecting fear or anger from Lincoln—maybe even a request to meet and make a deal. But instead, Lincoln elegantly called his bluff.

But this begs the obvious question: Did Allen really have any dirt on Lincoln? It's impossible to know. The historical record of Lincoln's early life is rather sparse. No one is perfect, and Lincoln might very well have made some mistakes in his life that he preferred to keep private. Let's say, for the sake of argument, that Lincoln had certain skeletons he wanted to keep in his closet. Was there any way for him to be absolutely sure that Allen had discovered those skeletons? No. If Lincoln had secrets, maybe Allen had discovered them; maybe not. And if Lincoln didn't have any secrets to hide, how could he have proven that he wasn't hiding anything? So at the end of the day, it didn't really matter if Allen was telling the truth. What mattered was how Lincoln responded.

3. **Lincoln focused on the one thing he had control over.** When you find yourself the target of unfair accusations or rumors—or even when someone is just treating you like crap for no good reason—you can't control how *they* choose to act. You can't force *them* to stop calling you bad names. Lincoln understood this. So he focused on the one thing that he did have control over: *his* reaction. He could have responded to Allen's despicable actions by firing off a letter filled with equally despicable language. Again, that would have played into Allen's hands, and likely escalated the situation into something far nastier

(and perhaps more public).

So instead, Lincoln contrasted his behavior to Allen's. Where Allen had been scurrilous, Lincoln would be gracious. Where Allen had been malicious, Lincoln would be respectful. He wrote the letter as if his own mother would read it. The next time you feel the urge to fire off an angry email to someone, you might try the same trick—it works.

4. **He appealed to Allen's emotions**. Lincoln no doubt surprised Allen by complimenting and flattering him. Instead of lashing out in anger—which, again, might have been exactly what Allen wanted—Lincoln responded to his attacker gravely and soberly. He even played on Allen's emotions, assuring him that if he did make public what he knew (or thought he knew) about Lincoln, he would still consider himself Allen's friend. You can almost hear the violins playing in the background! But beneath this gracious and humble sentiment is a rock-solid resolve. Between the lines, Lincoln is telling

Allen: *I won't do what you want. I won't sink to your level by calling you names. You cannot intimidate me.*

By responding calmly, without a trace of fear or rancor, Lincoln proved his strength. Note, too, the last line of the letter: "I wish an answer to this, and you are at liberty to publish both, if you choose." In other words, *I'm not afraid of you. And if you want to show everyone this letter, go ahead. I don't care.*

Elegant. Graceful. Tough as leather.

Oh, and in case you're wondering: Allen never responded to the letter, and there is no record that he ever leaked any damaging information about Lincoln… who, incidentally, won his bid for reelection.

CHAPTER 2

Clearing the Air after an Argument

WHO HASN'T GOTTEN INTO AN ARGUMENT with someone they didn't like? In the fall of 1840, Lincoln, then thirty-one years old, found himself in that situation with Dr. W.G. Anderson, who was running against Lincoln for a seat in the state legislature. The two got into a very heated—and public—dispute on the campaign trail. A few days later, Anderson wrote him a brief letter:

Dear Sir,

On our first meeting, on Wednesday last, a difficulty in words ensued between us, which I deem it my duty to notice further. I think you were the aggressor. Your words imported insult, and whether you meant them as such is for you to say. You will

therefore please inform me on this point, and if you designed to
offend me, please communicate to me your present feelings on
the subject, and whether you persist in the stand you took.
  Your obedient servant,
  W. G. Anderson

Basically, Anderson is telling Lincoln: "You started it. You insulted me, and now I'm giving you a chance to explain yourself." It's written in a haughty and condescending tone.

So how did Lincoln respond? It's not so much what he wrote, but what he didn't write. His brief reply is a textbook example of maintaining one's cool.

LETTER TO W. G. ANDERSON, LAWRENCEVILLE, ILLINOIS (OCTOBER 31, 1840)

Dear Sir,
Your note of yesterday is received. In the difficulty between
us of which you speak, you say you think I was the aggressor.
I do not think I was. You say my "words imported insult."
I meant them as a fair set-off to your own statements, and
not otherwise; and in that light alone I now wish you to

understand them. You ask for my present "feelings on the subject." I entertain no unkind feelings to you, and none of any sort upon the subject, except a sincere regret that I permitted myself to get into such an altercation.

On first reading, this may appear to be a bland, unremarkable response—but that's the whole point.

1. **Lincoln didn't escalate the conflict by lashing back at Anderson.** Instead, he poured cold water on the fire by responding quickly and calmly to Anderson's letter—no insults, no name-calling. Look at the short sentences and note how he addressed Anderson's main arguments logically and almost dispassionately: *You think I was the aggressor? I disagree. You thought I insulted you? I was responding to what you said.* And then he ended it by saying, in effect: *Look, I'm not mad at you, and I'm sorry the whole thing happened. Period. End of story.*

2. **Lincoln maintained a cool professionalism.** While effective, Lincoln's response is also rather

cold; you can tell there's no love lost between himself and Anderson. But is that such a bad thing? After all, the two weren't friends; they were political enemies. If Lincoln had responded warmly, he probably would have come off as fake and smarmy—a typical politician. He didn't feel the need to emphasize his dislike for Anderson, but neither did he try to disguise it by pouring on false charm.

3. **Lincoln wrote the letter as if other people would read it.** Whenever you communicate with an enemy—even if it's in a private letter or email—you have to write as if the whole world is watching. Why? Because if you make a mistake and write something inappropriate, you can be sure that your enemy will make it public. Lincoln no doubt realized this, which is another reason why he kept his response short and sweet. Reread it. Is there anything in it that you find objectionable, or that could have been used against him in his reelection bid? Not a thing. By responding in a simple yet

professional manner, he managed to not only avoid a scandal, but also made Anderson appear to be more than a little foolish and thin-skinned for dragging out their disagreement and seeking an apology.

CHAPTER 3

Turning Down a Relative's Request for Money

THERE ARE UNCOMFORTABLE SITUATIONS AND then there are *really* uncomfortable situations—like when a relative asks to borrow money. Lincoln faced that situation in 1851 when his stepbrother, John D. Johnston, made one of his frequent requests for a loan. The two had grown up together in Illinois in a tiny log cabin, but developed vastly different temperaments. Johnston had, in the words of Lincoln historian Charles Washington Moores, "the restless, thriftless irresponsibility of the chronic emigrant who fancied he could gain social betterment without working for it."

Responding to such a request in the right way is only slightly more complicated than disarming an atomic bomb. But once again, Lincoln's innate wisdom and writing skills shone through. His response:

LETTER TO JOHN D. JOHNSTON (JANUARY 2, 1851)

Dear Johnston,

Your request for eighty dollars I do not think it best to comply with now. At the various times when I have helped you a little you have said to me, "We can get along very well now"; but in a very short time I find you in the same difficulty again. Now, this can only happen by some defect in your conduct. What that defect is, I think I know. You are not lazy, and still you are an idler. I doubt whether, since I saw you, you have done a good whole day's work in any one day. You do not very much dislike to work, and still you do not work much, merely because it does not seem to you that you could get much for it. This habit of uselessly wasting time is the whole difficulty; it is vastly impor-tant to you, and still more so to your children, that you should break the habit. It is more important to them, because they have longer to live, and can keep out of an idle habit before they are in it, easier than they can get out after they are in.

You are now in need of some money; and what I propose is, that you shall go to work, "tooth and nail," for somebody who will give you money for it. Let father and your boys take charge of your things at home, prepare for a crop, and make the crop, and you go to work for the best money wages, or in discharge of any debt you owe, that you can get; and, to secure you a fair reward for your labour, I now promise you, that for every dollar you will, between this and the first of May, get for your own labour, either in money or as your own indebtedness, I will then give you one other dollar. By this, if you hire yourself at ten dollars a month, from me you will get ten more, making twenty dollars a month for your work. In this I do not mean you shall go off to St. Louis, or the lead mines, or the gold mines in California, but I mean for you to go at it for the best wages you can get close to home in Coles County.

Now, if you will do this, you will be soon out of debt, and, what is better, you will have a habit that will keep you from getting in debt again. But, if I should now clear you out of debt, next year you would be just as deep in as ever. You say you would almost give your place in heaven for seventy or eighty dollars. Then you value your place in heaven very cheap, for I am sure you can, with the offer I make, get the seventy or eighty dollars for four or five months' work. You say if I will furnish you the money you will deed me the land, and, if you don't pay the money back, you will deliver possession.

Nonsense! If you can't now live with the land, how will you then live without it? You have always been kind to me, and I do not mean to be unkind to you. On the contrary, if you will but follow my advice, you will find it worth more than eighty times eighty dollars to you.

What lessons can we learn here? How can you respond effectively in a similar situation?

1. **Lincoln got right to the point.** We'll see this repeatedly throughout Lincoln's correspondence: there was no beating around the bush, no pleasantries, no "Hey, how are the wife and kids? What's the weather like back home?" If Lincoln had started out this way, it would have shown he was uncomfortable or, worse, indecisive about his brother's request. But it also would have been a waste of time (and ink). Neither Lincoln nor his stepbrother was interested in talking about little things. John had asked him for eighty dollars—a sizeable chunk of change in those days. Lincoln, by addressing the matter in the opening sentence and rejecting

the request, shows that he is firm and in control of the situation. The strong opening also tells John, in effect, *I've made up my mind on this, so don't try to argue.*

2. **Lincoln controlled his emotions.** This wasn't the first time his stepbrother had asked for money, and Lincoln was no doubt incredibly frustrated by the situation. But he didn't lose his cool and start calling his brother every name in the book (although he probably felt like it!). He knew that it might feel good to vent at his stepbrother, but it wouldn't solve anything. In fact, it would only make matters much worse. Lincoln was doing more than simply responding to a request for money; he was also trying to keep peace in his family.

3. **Lincoln's tone was firm, but not berating.** Lincoln rejected his brother's loan request swiftly and firmly. However, once that was accomplished, he didn't go on a long rant about his brother's character flaws. Rather, he moved on to make his

case for turning down the request with a blunt, honest explanation. The important point here is that Lincoln wasn't afraid to tell the truth and risk hurting his brother's feelings—but he did so in the quickest and most honest way he could.

4. **Lincoln mixed a little honey with the vinegar.** After he broke the bad news to John, Lincoln went on to explain his reasoning, and softened the blow by telling him, "You are not lazy, and still you are an idler...You do not very much dislike to work, and still you do not work much, merely because it does not seem to you that you could get much for it."

Translation: *Look, you're not a terrible guy, but you definitely have some problems that you need to work on.*

Lincoln then made a very crafty rhetorical move: he pulled the focus away from the two of them and focused on John's children. "This habit of uselessly wasting time is the whole difficulty; it is vastly important to you, and still more so to your children, that you should break the habit. It is more important to them, because they have longer to live, and can keep out of an idle habit before they are in it, easier than they can get out after they are in."

Translation: *This isn't personal. This isn't about me telling you how to live your life. This is about doing what's right for your kids.*

5. **Lincoln offered a constructive alternative.** Rather than just saying no to John's loan request and leaving it at that, Lincoln came back with a counteroffer and an incentive. He told his stepbrother that merely giving him the money wouldn't really solve anything; however, if John got a job, Lincoln promised to match his wages, dollar for dollar, until he was out of debt.

This was not only generous—it was smart. He left the door open to helping John while simultaneously quashing any complaints that he didn't want to part with his own money.

No record exists of John's reply to Lincoln, so we don't know what decision he ultimately made (however, judging by the next chapter, it's obvious John continued to have problems). Regardless, we can learn a lot about how to deal with exasperating relatives from Lincoln's firm yet loving letter.

CHAPTER 4

Giving Advice to a Close Relative

THERE IS PERHAPS NO GREATER TEMPTATION than telling our close relatives what they should do with their lives. We've all been there—and Abraham Lincoln was no exception. It's always a tricky proposition, especially when the relatives in question are fully grown adults. Should we mind our own business, or give them the benefit of our vast storehouse of knowledge and wisdom?

There's no easy answer. But if you do decide to speak up and give your relative some advice—as Lincoln did—you can learn a lot from his approach.

To set the scene: it's November 1851. It's been ten months since Lincoln's stepbrother, John, asked for a loan (see previous chapter), and he apparently still hasn't learned his lesson.

LETTER TO JOHN D. JOHNSTON (NOVEMBER 4, 1851)

Dear Brother,

When I came into Charleston day before yesterday, I learned that you are anxious to sell the land where you live and move to Missouri. I have been thinking of this ever since, and cannot but think such a notion is utterly foolish. What can you do in Missouri better than here? Is the land any richer? Can you there, any more than here, raise corn and wheat and oats without work? Will anybody there, any more than here, do your work for you? If you intend to go to work, there is no better place than right where you are; if you do not intend to go to work, you cannot get along anywhere. Squirming and crawling about from place to place can do no good. You have raised no crop this year; and what you really want is to sell the land, get the money, and spend it. Part with the land you have, and, my life upon it, you will never after own a spot big enough to bury you in. Half you will get for the land you will spend in moving to Missouri, and the other half you will eat, drink, and wear out, and no foot of land will be bought.

Now, I feel it my duty to have no hand in such a piece of foolery. I feel that it is so even on your own account, and particularly on mother's account. The eastern forty acres I intend to keep for mother while she lives; if you will not cultivate it, it will rent for enough to support her—at least, it will rent for something. Her dower in the other two forties she can let you have, and no thanks to me.

Now, do not misunderstand this letter; I do not write it in any unkindness. I write it in order, if possible, to get you to face the truth, which truth is, you are destitute because you have idled away all your time. Your thousand pretences for not getting along better are all nonsense; they deceive nobody but yourself. Go[ing] to work is the only cure for your case.

C'mon, Abe, tell us what you really think!

This is the most forceful letter we've seen from Lincoln thus far. It's obvious he was exasperated with his stepbrother, and felt comfortable enough in his relationship with John to let that exasperation show through. But as we've seen before with Lincoln, he did not let his emotions overrule his intellect. While he was blunt, forceful, and direct with his brother, *he didn't lose his temper.* He expressed his displeasure without being displeasing. There's a big difference.

1. **Lincoln relied on facts and logic to bolster his argument, not emotion.** Rather than hurling a string of insults at his stepbrother and reinforcing his own negative reaction, Lincoln instead focused on building an argument against John's idea of selling his land and moving to Missouri.

   He didn't waste any time, either. Look at the beginning of the letter again:

   Sentence 1: *I hear you want to move to Missouri.*

   Sentence 2: *I think that's a foolish decision.*

   Sentences 3 through 11: *Here are my reasons.*

   Once again, we see Lincoln refusing to beat around the bush. After two quick introductory sentences that make clear his opinion, he moved straight into a barrage of counterarguments. For the next nine sentences, he peppered his stepbrother with apparently solid reasons against moving to Missouri.

After that barrage, he summarized, "Now, I feel it my duty to have no hand in such a piece of foolery." He waited until *after* he's made a logical and comprehensive argument to indulge in a bit of harsh language (well, harsh for 1851, anyway).

2. **He didn't end on a (completely) sour note.** After a brief discussion of their mother's property, Lincoln deliberately changed his tone, and ended with, "Now, do not misunderstand this letter; I do not write it in any unkindness."

    This may have seemed like cold comfort to John! But Lincoln knew the importance of stressing the fact that he was writing out of concern, not anger. He gave his stepbrother a dose of tough love: "Your thousand pretences for not getting along better are all nonsense; they deceive nobody but yourself."

So the next time your sister tells you she's quitting her job and moving to Oregon with her biker boyfriend, or your brother wants to pop the question to a stripper he met at a bar last weekend, and you absolutely cannot resist putting in your own two cents' worth, remember Lincoln's rules:

1. Don't lose your temper.
2. Don't belittle or insult the person you are advising.
3. Focus on facts and logic to bolster your argument, not emotion.
4. Get to the point quickly; be firm.
5. End on a positive note.

evening shortly after you were installed, and besought you that, so far as in your power, no man from Illinois should be appointed to any high office, without my being at least heard on the question. You were kind enough to say you thought my request a reasonable one. Mr. Butterfield is my friend, is well qualified, and, I suppose, would be faithful in the office. So far, good.

But now for the objections. In 1840 we fought a fierce and laborious battle in Illinois, many of us spending almost the entire year in the contest. The general victory came, and with it, the appointment of a set of drones, including this same Butterfield, who had never spent a dollar or lifted a finger in the fight. The place he got was that of District Attorney. The defection of Tyler came, and then B. played off and on, and kept the office till after Polk's election. Again, winter and spring before the last, when you and I were almost sweating blood to have Genl. Taylor nominated, this same man was ridiculing the idea, and going for Mr. Clay; and when Gen. T. was nominated, if he went out of the city of Chicago to aid in his election, it is more than I ever heard, or believe. Yet, when the election is secured, by other men's labor, and even against his effort, why, he is the first man on hand for the best office that our state lays any claim to. Shall this thing be?

CHAPTER 5

Handling a Sticky Situation

S OMETIMES YOU CAN'T AVOID LOOKING LIKE A jerk. It's one of the secrets of adulthood that no one ever tells you about beforehand. Sure, your parents teach you right and wrong, your college professors prepare you for the "real world," and your first boss helps you learn the ropes in your particular career field. You receive a constant stream of advice, but no one ever pulls you aside and lets you in on one of the biggest pitfalls of being a grown-up: doing the right thing and following your own conscience sometimes means making choices that not only anger your friends and co-workers, but can also make you look callous, self-serving, and just plain mean.

Abraham Lincoln found himself in this uncomfortable position more than once in his political career. The example below shows how he handled one such painful situation.

In the spring of 1849, Lincoln's political career was looking up. General Zachary Taylor, a Whig like Lincoln, had just been elected president, and party members were busy jockeying for position and vying for jobs in the new administration. One of the plum positions was the high-profile Commissioner of the General Land Office, who was responsible for the administration of public lands in the West. Justin Butterfield, a fellow Whig and Lincoln's friend, was being considered for the post. Although Lincoln had nothing personal against Butterfield, he didn't think he was the best person for the job, and initially supported another candidate, Cyrus Edwards. From the letters he wrote during that period, it's clear Lincoln felt that Butterfield hadn't worked hard enough for the party to deserve the job, and if he were awarded the choice post, it would severely weaken the morale of other young Whigs.

To make matters worse, after it became clear that Edwards didn't have a chance of securing the job,

Lincoln threw his own hat in the ring. Tal awkward: Although his reservations about Bu were no doubt sincere, others might think merely bad-mouthing his friend in order t the position for himself—and it was hard that Lincoln had ambitions of his own. Th dragged on for quite some time, and Linco numerous letters to Whig officials arguing h

As you can tell from the opening lines of below, Lincoln was clearly uncomfortable. ' end of the day, he believed that opposing Butt the right thing to do, even if it appeared self-

LETTER TO WILLIAM B. PREST (MAY 16, 1849)

Dear Sir:

It is a delicate matter to oppose the wishes of a consequently I address you on the subject I now little hesitation. Last night I received letters fr persons at Washington assuring me it was not that Justin Butterfield, of Chicago, Ills, would Commissioner of the Genl. Land-Office. It wa very thing, that I called on you at your room.

Our whigs will throw down their arms, and fight no more, if the fruit of their labor is thus disposed of. If there is one man in this state who desires B's appointment to any thing, I declare I have not heard of him. What influence operates for him, I can not conceive. Your position makes it a matter of peculiar interest to you, that the administration shall be successful; and be assured, nothing can more endanger it, than making appointments through old-hawker foreign influences, which offend, rather than gratify, the people immediately interested in the offices.

Can you not find time to write me, even half as long a letter as this? I shall be much gratified if you will.

Your Obt. Servt.

Lincoln was treading a very fine line. He had to lay out the reasons why he believed Butterfield was wrong for the General Land Office post without looking as if he was personally attacking or demeaning the man. Let's take a look at his rhetorical choices:

1. **He was up front about his feelings.** In the very first line, Lincoln acknowledged the difficulty of his task: "It is a delicate matter to oppose

the wishes of a friend." He instantly framed
the matter as one of utmost personal difficulty,
and identified Butterfield from the outset as a
friend, not an enemy.

2. **His criticisms were objective, not personal.**
When it comes time to cite his objections
against Butterfield, Lincoln never once leveled a
cheap shot or a personal insult against the man.
Instead, he soberly and unflinchingly listed
the reasons why he felt Butterfield should not
be given the post: he didn't work hard for the
party and ridiculed the idea of Taylor's nomination; thus, it would be unfair to reward him
with the post. Then he went one step further,
warning that other members of the party will
"throw down their arms, and fight no more" if
folks like Butterfield were rewarded for other
people's hard labors. In other words, he made it
about more than just his personal reservations.
He argued that the wrong move would be disastrous for the entire party. It was a great way to
preemptively fend off accusations that Lincoln
was only looking out for himself.

And reread that section again. Can you find any trace of personal animus against Butterfield? Lincoln was obviously frustrated by the situation, but he never let that frustration spill over into name-calling.

3. **Lincoln chose the Band-Aid approach.** You've heard the old adage that it's better to quickly rip off a Band-Aid from your skin and get it over with than to try to slowly peel it away. When you pull it off in one swift motion, there's a certain amount of pain, but nothing compared to what it feels like to have it lifted away inch by excruciating inch.

   The same principle applies when addressing an uncomfortable subject in a letter: best to get it over with quickly. We already noted Lincoln's habit of getting to the point right away. But note also how swiftly and economically he presented his objections to Butterfield. There were no personal asides, no apologies: he said what he had to say, and then he shut up. A short story writer once summed up his approach to telling a story as simply, "Get in, get out, keep moving."

The same wisdom can be applied to addressing a serious disagreement: say what you need to say firmly and with conviction, stay away from negative emotions, and *don't linger.*

(Oh, and in case you're wondering how it turned out: Lincoln failed in his bid, and Butterfield received the appointment to the General Land Office after all.)

CHAPTER 6

Taking Emotion out of the Equation

NY PROBLEM CAN QUICKLY BECOME EMOTIONALLY charged, regardless of whether it occurs in your personal or professional life. A co-worker you don't get along with criticizes your proposal for the firm's biggest client. Your ex-mother-in-law demands to see her grandchildren at a moment's notice. A neighbor complains about your dog tearing into his garbage. If these situations aren't handled in a calm, rational manner, tempers on both sides can flare and what started out as a run-of-the-mill disagreement can turn into a full-fledged war of words (or worse, fists).

Lincoln faced these kinds of obstacles on a daily basis, first as a lawyer in Illinois and through his time as president. Of course, the stakes were often much higher, and the problems much more complex, than those in our own day-to-day lives. But the strategies he used to deal with them one hundred fifty years ago are as fresh and relevant as ever.

Over the course of writing this book, I've pored over hundreds of Lincoln's letters, and the one thing that jumps out again and again is his consistent *tone*. Regardless of the situation, Lincoln was unfailingly calm, clear-headed, and concise; he didn't lose his cool easily. In fact, after searching through volume after volume of his correspondence from the 1830s through the 1860s, it's difficult to find even one example of Lincoln losing his temper. And believe me, he had plenty of opportunities to do just that. Throughout his political career, he was threatened, slandered, challenged, and excoriated on an almost daily basis.

So how did he do it? Was he a superhero? Of course not. And it wasn't just a matter of him gritting his teeth and pretending not to be angry or upset, either. As we'll see from the following examples, Lincoln didn't mask his emotions and put on a false front. Instead, he learned how to acknowledge his most extreme emotions but then set them aside so that he could deal with the issue at hand. It's a subtle but important difference, one that takes a certain amount of discipline. But if you can figure it out, you'll find that even the most irritating problems can be quickly defused in much the same way a bomb expert can avert an explosion by snipping a single wire on an explosive device. The act of cutting the wire is simple—the art comes in knowing which wire to cut.

Reaction vs. Response

Lincoln's letters—especially those written during tense times—are textbook examples of the difference between *responding* to a situation and merely *reacting* to it. Response takes thought, while *reaction* relies on simple hair-trigger emotions.

Think of it as a two-step process. The reaction always comes first. When you stub your toe on the coffee table, you react instantly by crying out in pain and maybe blurting out an expletive. When you accidentally touch a hot stove, you react by jerking your hand away (and maybe blurting out an expletive). When a loud noise awakens you in the middle of the night, your instant reaction is one of fear, even panic—your heart rate goes through the roof as your mind attempts to pull itself out of sleep mode and assess the danger.

Now imagine trying to solve a problem during any of these instances. Imagine, a millisecond after stubbing your toe on the coffee table, being asked to respond calmly and productively to criticism. Or imagine being called upon to deal with a crisis in the workplace five seconds after that mysterious noise wakes you up at two o'clock in the morning. Think you could do it? Of course not! When you're in the throes of automatic reaction mode, your emotions are dominant, your blood pressure is off the charts, and your sense of rationality has left the building.

But here's the good news: the wild emotions that you feel during this initial reaction phase inevitably fade away after a few seconds or minutes. Reaction is like the first stage of a rocket: it thrusts the space capsule through the atmosphere, but once its fuel has been spent, it's disconnected from the capsule and tumbles back to earth.

When you're confronted with a difficult situation and need to respond, the key is to wait for the first stage of the rocket—the initial rush of emotion—to fall away before saying or writing anything. The next time someone sends you an email that really pushes your buttons and you rush to compose a reply, think of stubbing your toe or burning your hand on the stove. You've just had the equivalent experience with a real person, the only difference being that they've hurt you emotionally, not physically. Resist the urge to give in to your emotions and react. In fact, it's this very act of resistance—of not doing anything at all—that allows you to move to the next stage.

A *response* is the second part of the process. It comes after the initial reaction has burned itself off. A response is more measured, less emotional. A response takes into account the bigger picture; its purpose is not to help you vent your emotions, but to attain the desired end goal, which can be anything from winning an argument, convincing someone not to take a certain action, or healing a rift and turning the enemy who attacked you into a friend. Whereas a reaction is unthinking and instinctive, a response is a strategic move that has been planned and thought out beforehand—not in order to manipulate the other person, but to ensure that you get your point across clearly and forcefully.

The person who chooses to respond rather than react is wise enough to realize that, while countering an attack with a knee-jerk emotional outburst or a fit of name-calling might feel good for a few seconds, it will also escalate the conflict. You poke me with a sharp stick, I'll poke you back with an even sharper one, and then you'll run off to find a bigger stick, and so on. The game continues but nothing gets accomplished, and as anyone who's ever watched a knock-down, drag-out argument between two grown adults in a professional setting can tell you, it won't improve your reputation among colleagues and supervisors, either.

Let's look at how Lincoln put this reaction/response principle into action. Take, for example, a public announcement that Lincoln wrote and had printed up as a flyer in the summer of 1846. He was once again in the throes of a campaign, and once again, his opponents were slinging mud at him. But this time, his enemies were striking a very low blow—spreading scurrilous rumors that he was hostile to Christianity.

In the United States of the 1840s, such a charge, if it caught hold, would sink a candidate for good (come to think of it, it would probably ruin a career today, too).

Talk about radioactive! Can you imagine how angry Lincoln must have been when he heard what was being said about him? Who did these guys think they were, questioning his faith and implying that he openly mocked churchgoers? The nerve! The audacity! I don't think it's too far-fetched to imagine Lincoln ranting and raving to his friends when he first found out. An ink jar or two might have been thrown against the wall of his office. After all, it's natural to react emotionally when you're unfairly attacked.

But when Lincoln calmed down—and it's important to stress that he let himself calm down before taking pen to paper—he went into *response* mode. Here is the full text of the handbill he wrote on July 31, 1846, responding to the rumors. See if you can notice the underlying principles of response vs. reaction here:

Handbill Replying to
Charges of Infidelity

To the Voters of the Seventh Congressional District

FELLOW CITIZENS:

A charge having got into circulation in some of the neighbor-hoods of this District, in substance that I am an open scoffer at Christianity, I have by the advice of some friends concluded to notice the subject in this form. That I am not a member of any Christian Church, is true; but I have never denied the truth of the Scriptures; and I have never spoken with intentional disrespect of religion in general, or of any denomination of Christians in particular. It is true that in early life I was inclined to believe in what I understand is called the "Doctrine of Necessity"—that is, that the human mind is impelled to action, or held in rest by some power, over which the mind itself has no control; and I have sometimes (with one, two, or three, but never publicly) tried to maintain this opinion in argument. The habit of arguing thus however, I have, entirely left off for more than five years. And I add here, I have always understood this same opinion to be held by several of the Christian denominations. The foregoing, is the whole truth, briefly stated, in relation to myself, upon this subject.

> *I do not think I could myself, be brought to support a man for office, whom I knew to be an open enemy of, and scoffer at, religion. Leaving the higher matter of eternal consequences, between him and his Maker, I still do not think any man has the right thus to insult the feelings, and injure the morals, of the community in which he may live. If, then, I was guilty of such conduct, I should blame no man who should condemn me for it; but I do blame those, whoever they may be, who falsely put such a charge in circulation against me.*

First off, let's talk about what we don't see in Lincoln's handbill: no sputtering rage. No vengeful attacks on his enemies. No name-calling. Instead, what we get is a strong, brief statement that exudes confidence and maturity. We get a response rather than a reaction.

This doesn't mean that Lincoln affected a cold, calculating tone—he let it be known that he was unhappy with what was being said ("I do blame those, whoever they may be, who falsely put such a charge in circulation against me"). But he was also mindful of the fact that the people reading his statement were the same ones he wanted to vote for him in the upcoming election. If he couldn't control his emotions during a rough-and-tumble campaign, why would they expect him to keep his cool after he was elected to office?

Lincoln answered the shadowy rumors with plain-spoken honesty. After a brief recap of the charges against him, he countered with a series of short factual statements: True, he didn't belong to a church, but neither had he denied the truth of the Bible or mocked other believers. Note, too, the length of Lincoln's response. He didn't go on for pages and pages trying to prove how religious he was. He didn't pore over the accusations and pick them apart in minute detail. Why not? It's a good guess that Lincoln knew a long, protracted response would only bring more attention to the allegations. Some might also wonder why he spent so much time and attention on the matter if the charges were, as he claimed, untrue. No, it was better to address the matter seriously, but only afford it two paragraphs. By doing so, Lincoln showed that he wasn't going to ignore his detractors, but he wasn't going to give them the satisfaction of overreacting to their accusations either.

Does this mean an effective response must always be pithy and brief? No. Depending on the situation and the intended audience, it may be necessary to devote significant time and attention to rebutting an attack. A few months before he responded to the anti-Christian rumors, in February 1846, Lincoln wrote a letter to General John J. Hardin, a politician and fellow member of the Whig Party. At the time, Lincoln was preparing to make a run for his party's nomination for election to the U.S. Congress. Hardin had already served a term in Congress and wanted to run again, and accused Lincoln of engaging in political maneuvering to edge him out. The politics of the time were complicated, but in short, Hardin said that Lincoln had acted rather sneakily to make sure that their party would nominate Lincoln to the congressional seat by spreading a rumor that Hardin was instead interested in running for governor. Hardin even managed to get a state newspaper to reprint his charges, albeit without mentioning his name (even in the 1840s, anonymous sources were already causing trouble!).

Rather than respond publicly, Lincoln decided to write Hardin a private—and very lengthy—letter in which he meticulously refuted his rival's charges point by point. The letter is too long to reprint in full—

and the in-depth discussion of nineteenth-century politics would probably put you to sleep—but by looking at a few key passages, we can learn some valuable lessons about keeping one's cool under pressure. Here's the opening:

LETTER TO GENERAL JOHN J. HARDIN (FEB. 7, 1846)

Dear Sir:

Your second letter was duly received and, so far as it goes, it is entirely satisfactory.

I had set apart the leisure this day affords, to write you the long letter alluded to by me in my last; but on going to the Post-office, and seeing the communication in the Morgan Journal, I am almost discouraged of the hope of doing any good by it; especially when I reflect that most probably that communication was written with your knowledge, in as much as it proceeds partly on information which could only have been furnished by you.

However, as I suppose it can do no harm, I will proceed. Your letter, admitting my right to seek, or desire, a nomination for congress, opens with an expression of dissatisfaction with the manner in which you think I have endeavoured to obtain it. Now, if I have, sought the nomination in an improper manner; you have the right, to the extent, to be dissatisfied. But I deny all impropriety on my part, in the matter.

By now, you're probably noticing a pattern. Lincoln affected the same tone as in the handbill—what might be called "cool honesty." He didn't lose his temper, but nevertheless, made it very clear at the outset that Hardin's charges against him were misguided ("I deny all impropriety on my part, in the matter").

Lincoln then dug into the meat of Hardin's accusations. A couple of pages later, he addressed the "Hardin for governor" controversy:

I now quote from your letter again. "You well knew I would not be a candidate for Governor. Yet during the fall courts, whilst I learn you were obtaining pledges from all the whigs you could to support you for the next candidate, my name was run up as a candidate for Governor by one of your friends under circumstances which now leave no room for doubt that the design was to keep my name out of view for congress, so that the whigs might be more easily influenced to commit themselves to go for you."

> *Now this is a direct imputation that I procured, or winked at, or in some way directly or indirectly, had a hand in, the nominating of you for Governor; and the imputation is, to the utmost hair-breadth of it, unjust. I never knew, or believed, or had any suspicion, that it was done, or was to be done, until it was out, had gone to Alton, and been commented upon in the Alton paper, and came back to Springfield [...] I went immediately to the Journal office, and told them it was my wish that they should not fall in with the nomination for Governor. They showed me a little paragraph, which they had already prepared, and which was published, and seen by you, as I suppose. [...] That I was wholly innocent and ignorant of that movement, I believe, if need be, I can prove more conclusively than is often in the power of man to prove any such thing.*

Notice how Lincoln defended himself here: not by lashing out at Hardin with his own accusations, but by stating in clear, simple language, essentially, "I didn't do what you said I did." He didn't get emotional; he didn't have to. He let his choice of words ("wholly innocent," "unjust") deliver the impact. You can tell he meant what he said—that he really felt it—but he didn't go overboard.

One of the defining characteristics of an effective response is that it is unambiguous and clear. Emotional reactions are often so wildly out of control that it's hard to figure out what the person is saying. There's a lot of powerful heat, but it's not an argument—it may not make any sense, and certainly won't help the person's case. By contrast, a concise, simply worded response always knows where it's going—it's like a locomotive gathering steam as it courses down the track. Clarity is power.

Never Let Them See You Rehearse

If you had the choice between watching a theater group rehearse a play for the very first time or waiting until their opening-night premiere to see them perform, which would you choose? Would you rather read the first draft of a complex mystery novel or wait until it's been polished and perfected by the author and his or her editor?

In both instances, most people would choose to wait. Watching a group of actors fumble through their lines with a new script might be interesting for a little while, but it wouldn't be very entertaining. And plowing through a four-hundred-page novel replete with misspellings and errors in plot and logic isn't the most exciting way to while away a couple of evenings.

The same is true with emails, letters, and face-to-face conversations. If someone attacks or criticizes you unfairly, don't give a rough-draft reaction. Instead, follow Lincoln's lead: take the time to settle your emotions (and it may only require a few minutes and a few deep, calming breaths) and deliver a well-rehearsed and thoughtful response.

CHAPTER 7

Encouraging and Consoling Friends

L INCOLN WAS A TALENTED POLITICIAN, MASTER war strategist and, of course, a great president. But he was also a wonderful friend, and that's plainly evident in the handful of personal letters that survive.

In the following letter to one of his best friends, Joshua Speed, he sought to encourage his friend about his upcoming marriage to a girl named Fanny. Speed, who, like Lincoln, was often prone to deep bouts of depression, was having doubts about whether he was doing the right thing. We don't know what specifically prompted Lincoln to write this letter, but it's clear Joshua was, to use a modern term, "freaking out" over the situation. Notice how Lincoln gently and thoughtfully encouraged his friend.

Letter to Joshua F. Speed
(January 30, 1842)

My Dear Speed,

Feeling, as you know I do, the deepest solicitude for the success of the enterprise you are engaged in [marriage], I adopt this as the last method I can adopt to aid you, in case (which God forbid!) you shall need any aid.

I do not place what I am going to say on paper because I can say it better that way than I could by word of mouth, but, were I to say it orally before we part, most likely you would forget it at the very time when it might do you some good. As I think it reasonable that you will feel very badly some time between this and the final consummation of your purpose, it is intended that you shall read this just at such a time.

Why I say it is reasonable that you will feel very badly yet, is because of three special causes added to the general one which I shall mention. The general cause is, that you are naturally of a nervous temperament; and this I say from what I have seen of you personally, and what you have told me concerning your mother at various times, and concerning your brother William at the time his wife died.

you, does not pertain to one in a thousand. It is out of this that the painful difference between you and the mass of the world springs.

I know what the painful point with you is at all times when you are unhappy; it is an apprehension that you do not love her as you should. What nonsense! How came you to court her? Was it because you thought she deserved it, and that you had given her reason to expect it? If it was for that why did not the same reason make you court Ann Todd, and at least twenty others of whom you can think, and to whom it would apply with greater force than to her?

Did you court her for her wealth? Why, you know she had none. But you say you reasoned yourself into it. What do you mean by that? Was it not that you found yourself unable to reason yourself out of it? Did you not think, and partly form the purpose, of courting her the first time you ever saw her or heard of her? What had reason to do with it at that early stage? There was nothing at that time for reason to work upon.

Whether she was moral, amiable, sensible, or even of good character, you did not, nor could then know, except, perhaps, you might infer the last from the company you found her in. All you then did or could know of her was her personal

The first special cause is your exposure to bad weather on your journey, which my experience clearly proves to be very severe on defective nerves. The second is the absence of all business and conversation of friends, which might divert your mind, give it occasional rest from the intensity of thought which will sometimes wear the sweetest idea threadbare and turn it to the bitterness of death. The third is the rapid and near approach of that crisis on which all your thoughts and feelings concentrate.

If from all these causes you shall escape and go through triumphantly, without another "twinge of the soul," I shall be most happily but most egregiously deceived. If, on the contrary, you shall, as I expect you will at sometime, be agonized and distressed, let me, who have some reason to speak with judgment on such a subject, beseech you to ascribe it to the causes I have mentioned, and not to some false and ruinous suggestion of the Devil.

"But," you will say, "do not your causes apply to every one engaged in alike undertaking?" By no means. The particular causes, to a greater or less extent, perhaps do apply in all cases; but the general one—nervous debility, which is the key and conductor of all the particular ones, and without whi they would be utterly harmless—though it does pertain *appearance and deportment; and these, if they impress at all, impress the heart, and not the head. Say candidly, were not those heavenly black eyes the whole basis of all your early reasoning on the subject? After you and I had once been at the residence, did you not go and take me all the way to Lexington and back, for no other purpose but to get to see her again, on our return on that evening to take a trip for that express object?*

What earthly consideration would you take to find her scouting and despising you, and giving herself up to another? But of this you have no apprehension; and therefore you cannot bring it home to your feelings. I shall be so anxious about you that I shall want you to write by every mail.

Your friend,

Lincoln

What does this letter teach us about how to better encourage our own friends during times of trouble?

1. **Lincoln created a sharp contrast between his own attitude and Joshua's.** This may seem elementary, but it's worth pointing out. Lincoln

had just received a panicky letter from his best friend. So how did he choose to respond—with an equally panicky reply? No. He knew that by doing so, he would only inflame the situation and possibly push his friend over the edge.

Lincoln didn't respond in frustration or anger, either (though he was probably feeling a little of both). He knew that the only way to reach his friend and calm him down was by being calm himself.

2. **Lincoln used gentle logic to make his friend feel better.** To convince Joshua that things weren't as bad as he thought, Lincoln asked questions to which the answers were obvious. Joshua seemed to be concerned that his feelings for Fanny weren't genuine ("I know what the painful point with you is at all times when you are unhappy; it is an apprehension that you do not love her as you should. What nonsense!"). So Lincoln poked holes in that assumption, pointing out how attracted Joshua was to Fanny; how he didn't feel the same way

toward many other girls; and how he wasn't courting her for material gain.

3. **Lincoln was blunt.** As we have seen in other examples of Lincoln's correspondence, he was a master at writing in a blunt but polite manner. Here we see that skill in action yet again. He began the letter by being absolutely honest with Joshua and noting that, like other members of his family, he had a "nervous temperament" and was prone to irrational anxiety. Lincoln even went so far as to anticipate in which situations Joshua would be liable to feel such anxiety, so that he could better prepare himself when it happens. It's almost as if he was writing him a prescription for antidepressants!

Lincoln's tactic worked—Joshua Speed married Fanny shortly thereafter. But Lincoln wasn't finished trying to help his friend cope with personal demons. The next month, he wrote the following:

LETTER TO JOSHUA F. SPEED
(FEBRUARY 13, 1842)

Dear Speed,

[Your letter] came to hand three or four days ago. When this shall reach you, you will have been Fanny's husband several days. You know my desire to befriend you is everlasting; that I will never cease while I know how to do anything. But you will always hereafter be on ground that I have never occupied, and consequently, if advice were needed, I might advise wrong. I do fondly hope, however, that you will never again need any comfort from abroad. But should I be mistaken in this, should excessive pleasure still be accompanied with a painful counterpart at times, still let me urge you, as I have ever done, to remember, in the depth and even agony of despondency, that very shortly you are to feel well again.

I am now fully convinced that you love her as ardently as you are capable of loving. Your ever being happy in her presence, and your intense anxiety about her health, if there were nothing else, would place this beyond all dispute in my mind. I incline to think it probable that your nerves will fail you occasionally for awhile; but once you get them firmly guarded now that trouble is over forever.

I think, if I were you, in case my mind were not exactly right, I would avoid being idle. I would immediately engage in some business, or go to making preparations for it, which would be the same thing. If you went through the ceremony calmly, or even with sufficient composure not to excite alarm in any present, you are safe beyond question, and in two or three months, to say the most, will be the happiest of men.

I would desire you to give my particular respects to Fanny; but perhaps you will not wish her to know you have received this, lest she should desire to see it. Make her write me an answer to my last letter to her; at any rate I would set great value upon a note or letter from her. Write me whenever you have leisure.

Yours forever,

A. Lincoln

P. S.—I have been quite a man since you left.

We see here that even though Lincoln had helped his friend calm his anxieties and marry Fanny, there was still work to be done! In this follow-up letter, Lincoln bolstered Joshua's confidence by assuring him that things would start looking up. He further attempted to boost his friend's morale by giving his own seal of

approval, telling Joshua, "I am now fully convinced
that you love her as ardently as you are capable of
loving." This is important; Lincoln was obviously
someone whom Joshua looked up to and admired.

Lincoln sought to encourage many other people, as
well. In the following classic letter to teenager George
Latham, a good friend of his son Robert, the president
consoles him for failing to gain admission to Harvard
University. George's father had died a few years earlier,
and it's obvious that Lincoln cared deeply about the boy.

LETTER TO GEORGE LATHAM
(JULY 22, 1860)

My dear George,

*I have scarcely felt greater pain in my life than on learning
yesterday from Bob's letter, that you had failed to enter Harvard
University. And yet there is very little in it, if you will allow no
feeling of discouragement to seize, and prey upon you.*

*It is a certain truth, that you can enter, and graduate in,
Harvard University; and having made the attempt, you must
succeed in it. "Must" is the word. I know not how to aid you,
save in the assurance of one of mature age, and much severe*

experience, that you can not fail, if you resolutely determine, that you will not.

The President of the institution, can scarcely be other than a kind man; and doubtless he would grant you an interview, and point out the readiest way to remove, or overcome, the obstacles which have thwarted you. In your temporary failure there is no evidence that you may not yet be a better scholar, and a more successful man in the great struggle of life, than many others, who have entered college more easily.

Again I say let no feeling of discouragement prey upon you, and in the end you are sure to succeed.

This is a model letter for anyone seeking to encourage a friend who's just suffered a great disappointment, especially someone younger than you are.

Lincoln's words are genuine because he obviously spoke from experience. His rise from a lowly log cabin to the presidency of the United States is the stuff of legend. There was no need for him to recount his life story to George, because George already knew it; thus, his words have an added power. Lincoln was someone who was not born into greatness; he earned it by applying the principles he laid out in the letter.

The older we get the more experience we amass, and are better able to pass on the lessons we learn to those younger than we are. Here is one final example from Lincoln's life. In 1862, his old friend William McCullough was killed in one of the early battles of the Civil War. Lincoln, who had known McCullough since his young lawyering days in Illinois, penned a letter of consolation to McCullough's daughter, Fanny:

LETTER TO FANNY
(DECEMBER 23, 1862)

Dear Fanny,

It is with deep grief that I learn of the death of your kind and brave Father; and, especially, that it is affecting your young heart beyond what is common in such cases.

In this sad world of ours, sorrow comes to all; and, to the young, it comes with bitterest agony, because it takes them unawares. The older have learned to ever expect it. I am anxious to afford some alleviation of your present distress. Perfect relief is not possible, except with time.

You can not now realize that you will ever feel better. Is not this so? And yet it is a mistake. You are sure to be happy again. To know this, which is certainly true, will make you some less miserable now. I have had experience enough to know what I say; and you need only to believe it, to feel better at once. The memory of your dear Father, instead of an agony, will yet be a sad sweet feeling in your heart, of a purer and holier sort than you have known before.

Please present my kind regards to your afflicted mother.
Your sincere friend,
A. Lincoln

There is great power in brevity. Notice how Lincoln quickly turned from offering his condolences to assuring Fanny that things would soon get better. He didn't want to make her feel any worse by reminding her of how wonderful her father was; his goal, once again, was to encourage someone much younger than himself by offering the benefit of his experience.

CHAPTER 8

Standing Your Ground in Difficult Circumstances

It's 1861: the early days of the Civil War. Lincoln—not to mention the entire country—is facing an incredibly daunting challenge. As the president tries to cobble together support and keep a fragile Union in one piece, Beriah Magoffin, the contentious governor of Kentucky, attempts to throw a wrench in his plans. Magoffin, a pro-slavery Confederate sympathizer, is angry that Union troops are beginning to organize in his state, and writes Lincoln a letter demanding that the soldiers leave.

Although the stakes are extremely high, and Magoffin easily has the power to disrupt Lincoln's plans for keeping the country united, the president's response is a masterpiece: calm, controlled, and unwavering.

Letter to Governor Magoffin
(August 24, 1861)

To His Excellency B. Magoffin, Governor of the State of Kentucky.

Sir:

Your letter of the 19th Inst., in which you urge the "removal from the limits of Kentucky of the military force now organized and in camp within that State," is received.

I may not possess full and precisely accurate knowledge upon this subject; but I believe it is true that there is a military force in camp within Kentucky, acting by authority of the United States, which force is not very large, and is not now being augmented.

I also believe that some arms have been furnished to this force by the United States.

I also believe this force consists exclusively of Kentuckians, having their camp in the immediate vicinity of their own homes, and not assailing or menacing any of the good people of Kentucky.

In all I have done in the premises I have acted upon the urgent solicitation of many Kentuckians, and in accordance with what I believed, and still believe, to be the wish of a majority of all the Union-loving people of Kentucky.

While I have conversed on this subject with many eminent men of Kentucky, including a large majority of her members of Congress, I do not remember that any one of them, or any other person, except your Excellency and the bearers of your Excellency's letter, has urged me to remove the military force from Kentucky or to disband it. One other very worthy citizen of Kentucky did solicit me to have the augmenting of the force suspended for a time.

Taking all the means within my reach to form a judgment, I do not believe it is the popular wish of Kentucky that this force shall be removed beyond her limits; and, with this impression, I must respectfully decline to so remove it.

I most cordially sympathize with your Excellency in the wish to preserve the peace of my own native State, Kentucky. It is with regret I search, and cannot find, in your not very short letter, any declaration or intimation that you entertain any desire for the preservation of the Federal Union.

Your obedient servant,

LINCOLN

Here we find Lincoln employing some familiar—and quite effective—strategies. Again, consider the actual situation: a state governor is presuming to tell the president what to do. Magoffin is demanding that the gathering of Union troops—made up of Kentucky residents, no less—be disbanded. If you were in Lincoln's shoes, what would be your initial reaction? Incredulity? Anger?

For all we know, that might have been Lincoln's first reaction as well. It would even have been justified. But that's not what he chose to put down on paper.

1. **Lincoln kept his emotions—and his ego—out of it.** Lincoln knew that showing excessive emotion—anger, rage, even hurt feelings or confusion—would be the equivalent of handing his enemy a figurative sword and inviting him to use it. More often than not, a display of raw emotion doesn't scare or weaken your opponent; it weakens your own position and makes you appear ineffective, even irrational. This is especially true if you're in a position of authority (like Lincoln) and the person attempting to disrupt your plans is your subordinate, or someone who is nominally under your authority (like Magoffin). If they don't respect you in the first place, blowing your top certainly isn't going to

help—in fact, it will give them another reason to despise you. Donald Trump may be able to throw a screaming fit every time something doesn't go his way and swear at everyone in the boardroom, but he's the exception to the rule (or should I say, his bank account is the exception!). If his entire executive team quit, he could replace them within twenty-four hours. Lincoln didn't have that luxury. He had power in the sense that he was president of the United States, but that power was being tested mightily by the Civil War, and many people—including Magoffin—were seeking to undermine his authority. And given the fragile political situation, they had a good chance of succeeding.

Note: That doesn't mean it's always wrong to make others aware of your displeasure with a situation, nor does it mean that anyone who shows a flash of anger is necessarily weakening his or her position. But excessive displays of emotion are almost always counterproductive, especially in tense, high-stakes situations.

2. **Lincoln relied on logic and facts.** In this instance, Lincoln took the opposite approach to blowing his top. You might call it the "Spock gambit." Spock, of course, was the emotionless, always logical Vulcan played by Leonard Nimoy on the classic sci-fi TV show *Star Trek*. Spock relied on cold, hard facts and data to make his decisions and win arguments with the emotional Dr. "Bones" McCoy.

Lincoln did the same thing with Magoffin. Look again at the opening of the letter: he began not with fire, but ice, reciting a long list of facts about the situation on which they could both agree. Magoffin's heated demands are met with rhetorical cold water.

After the facts had been established, Lincoln moved to the next phase of his argument: isolating Magoffin and pointing out that many prominent people in the state agree with Lincoln's position. "In all I have done in the premises I have acted upon the urgent solicitation of many Kentuckians," he began, going on to point out that he had spoken with "many eminent men of Kentucky," including several state lawmakers, and none of them said anything about removing the troops. "I do not believe it is the popular wish of Kentucky that this force shall be removed beyond her limits," he concluded, "and, with this impression, I must respectfully decline to so remove it." Again, Lincoln was relying on facts—or, at the very least, his own impressions based on discussions with other Kentuckians.

He ended the letter with a beautiful paragraph that served not only to chastise Magoffin, but also to reinforce Lincoln's own position:

> I most cordially sympathize with your Excellency in the wish to preserve the peace of my own native State, Kentucky. It is with regret I search, and cannot find, in your not very short letter, any declaration or intimation that you entertain any desire for the preservation of the Federal Union.

In other words, Lincoln said, *"I'm looking at the big picture. You're only interested in your own little state."* Another way to say it might be, *"You're thinking like a governor. I'm thinking like a president."* It's a devastating closing—a *coup de grace* executed not with rancor and blind emotion, but the cool exactitude of a professional leader. (It's also very clever—and it's impossible to be clever when you're seething.)

Next, we see Lincoln sticking to his guns in what had to have been an awkward and painful situation— turning down a request for reinstatement from a former officer with a checkered service record whose son had recently been killed in battle.

Letter to Major John Key
(Nov. 24, 1862)

Dear Sir:

A bundle of letters including one from yourself, was, early last week, handed me by Gen. Halleck, as I understood, at your request. I sincerely sympathize with you in the death of your brave and noble son.

In regard to my dismissal of yourself from the military service, it seems to me you misunderstand me. I did not charge, or intend to charge you with disloyalty. I had been brought to fear that there was a class of officers in the army, not very inconsiderable in numbers, who were playing a game to not beat the enemy when they could, on some peculiar notion as to the proper way of saving the Union; and when you were proved to me, in your own presence, to have avowed yourself in favor of that "game," and did not attempt to controvert the proof, I dismissed you as an example and a warning to that supposed class. I bear you no ill will; and I regret that I could not have the example without wounding you personally. But can I now, in view of the public interest, restore you to the service, by which the army would understand that I endorse and approve that game myself? If there was any doubt of your having made the avowal, the case would be different. But when it was proved to me, in your presence, you did not deny or attempt to deny it, but confirmed it in my mind, by attempting to sustain the position by argument.

I am really sorry for the pain the case gives you, but I do not see how, consistently with duty, I can change it.

Lincoln's strong sense of loyalty is also evident in his letters. In the following example, he wrote to Isaac Arnold, a personal friend and member of the House of Representatives, to stand up for one of his beleaguered military officers. Instead of giving in to popular political sentiment—and the wishes of a friend—Lincoln quietly but firmly refused to budge.

LETTER TO ISAAC ARNOLD
(MAY 26, 1863)

My dear Sir:

*Your letter advising me to dismiss Gen. Halleck is received.
If the public believe, as you say, that he has driven Fremont,
Butler, and Sigel from the service, they believe what I know
to be false; so that if I were to yield to it, it would only be
to instantly beset by some other demand based on another
falsehood equally gross. You know yourself that Fremont was
relieved at his own request, before Halleck could have had
any thing to do with it—went out near the end of June, while
Halleck only came in near the end of July. I know equally well
that no wish of Halleck's had anything to do with the removal
of Butler or Sigel. Sigel, like Fremont, was relieved at his own
request, pressed upon me almost constantly for six months,
and upon complaints that could have been made as justly by
almost any corps commander in the army, and more justly by
some. So much for the way they got out.*

*Now a word as to their not getting back. In the early Spring,
Gen. Fremont sought active service again; and, as it seemed
to me, sought it in a very good, and reasonable spirit. But
he holds the highest rank in the Army, except McClellan, so*

that I could not well offer him a subordinate command. Was I to displace Hooker, or Hunter, or Rosecrans, or Grant, or Banks? If not, what was I to do? And similar to this, is the case of both the others. One month after Gen. Butler's return, I offered him a position in which I thought and still think, he could have done himself the highest credit, and the country the greatest service, but he declined it. When Gen. Sigel was relieved, at his own request as I have said, of course I had to put another in command of his corps. Can I instantly thrust that other out to put him in again?

And now my good friend, let me turn your eyes upon another point. Whether Gen. Grant shall or shall not consummate the capture of Vicksburg, his campaign from the beginning of this month up to the twenty second day of it, is one of the most brilliant in the world. His corps commanders, & Division commanders, in part, are McClernand, McPherson, Sherman, Steele, Hovey, Blair, & Logan. And yet taking Gen. Grant & those seven of his generals, and you can scarcely name one of them that has not been constantly denounced and opposed by the same men who are now so anxious to get Halleck out, and Fremont & Butler & Sigel in. I believe no one of them went through the Senate easily, and certainly one failed to get through at all. I am compelled to take a more *impartial and unprejudiced view of things. Without claiming to be your superior, which I do not, my position enables me to understand my duty in all these matters better than you possibly can, and I hope you do not yet doubt my integrity. Your friend, as ever.*

The next time you find yourself compelled to respond to a nasty email or someone who questions your judgment, think of Lincoln sitting at his desk in the White House in the opening months of the Civil War. Pressure? High stakes? We don't know the meaning of those words! And yet he managed to deal with his critics' machinations without losing his head. So before responding, take a deep breath. Take two or three if you have to. Then get down to the business of defending yourself and standing your ground calmly and rationally. After all, that's how people expect leaders to act. If Abe could do it, so can we.

Finding the Humanity in Your Enemies

THROUGHOUT HIS POLITICAL CAREER, LINCOLN chose to mainly criticize the *institution* of slavery rather than those who *supported* slavery. He did this for a very simple reason: in order to one day become president, he would need the support of a broad coalition, and once in the office, he would need to continue to work to bring people together rather than widen the already deep divisions in the country.

In today's political culture, it's considered normal to lash out at one's ideological opponents and cast them in the worst light possible. But throughout Lincoln's speeches and official writings on slavery, he consistently reached out to his political and ideological opposites and acknowledged the difficulty of the problem. Read these excerpts from an 1854 debate against Senator Douglas in Peoria, Illinois:

...I hate [the spread of slavery] because of the monstrous injustice of slavery itself. I hate it because it deprives our republican example of its just influence in the world, enables the enemies of free institutions with plausibility to taunt us as hypocrites, causes the real friends of freedom to doubt our sincerity, and especially because it forces so many good men amongst ourselves into an open war with the very fundamental principles of civil liberty, criticizing the Declaration of Independence, and insisting that there is no right principle of action but self-interest.

Before proceeding, let me say I think I have no prejudice against the Southern people. They are just what we would be in their situation. If slavery did not now exist among them, they would not introduce it. If it did now exist among us, we should not instantly give it up. This I believe of the masses North and South. Doubtless there are individuals on both sides who would not hold slaves under any circumstances, and others who would gladly introduce slavery anew if it were out of existence. We know that some Southern men do free their slaves, go North and become tip-top abolitionists, while some Northern ones go South and become most cruel slave-masters.

When Southern people tell us they are no more responsible for the origin of slavery than we are, I acknowledge the fact. When it is said that the institution exists, and that it is very difficult to get rid of it in any satisfactory way, I can understand and appreciate the saying. I surely will not blame them for not doing what I should not know how to do myself. If all earthly power were given me, I should not know what to do as to the existing institution. My first impulse would be to free all the slaves, and send them to Liberia, to their own native land. But a moment's reflection would convince me that whatever of high hope (as I think there is) there may be in this in the long run, its sudden execution is impossible. If they were all landed there in a day, they would all perish in the next ten days; and there are not surplus shipping and surplus money enough to carry them there in many times ten days. What then? Free them all, and keep them among us as underlings?

...Equal justice to the South, it is said, requires us to consent to the extension of slavery to new countries. That is to say, that inasmuch as you do not object to my taking my hog to Nebraska, therefore I must not object to your taking

> *your slave. Now, I admit that this is perfectly logical, if there is no difference between hogs and slaves. But while you thus require me to deny the humanity of the negro, I wish to ask whether you of the South, yourselves, have ever been willing to do as much? It is kindly provided that of all those who come into the world, only a small percentage are natural tyrants. That percentage is no larger in the slave States than in the free. The great majority, South as well as North, have human sympathies, of which they can no more divest themselves than they can of their sensibility to physical pain. These sympathies in the bosoms of the Southern people manifest in many ways their sense of the wrong of slavery, and their consciousness that, after all, there is humanity in the negro.*

Notice how Lincoln stressed the commonalities, not differences, between Northerners and Southerners, anti-slavery and pro-slavery. He went out of his way to paint his opponents as reasonable people and was the first to admit that he didn't have all the answers. He wanted to change their minds about slavery, and he knew he couldn't accomplish that by calling them names.

So what does this have to do with our modern lives? Plenty. We may not find ourselves running for political office or engaging in great public debates on the issues of the day, but we will almost always find ourselves facing some sort of conflict, however small: a dispute with a co-worker, a disagreement with a friend, an ongoing argument with a spouse or romantic partner. Regardless of the specific situation, sooner or later you have to ask yourself: Do I want to make an effort to end this conflict, or do I want it to continue? If you want it to end, that means changing your strategy and stopping your knee-jerk, emotional reactions to the other person's words or actions (and the other person, by the way, believes that they're reacting to *you!*).

But be forewarned: choosing to end a conflict is never fun. It's much more entertaining to keep on fighting. You can wrap yourself in warm, cozy feelings of self-pity and think of yourself as a poor victim of a mean person (and who could ever dislike a victim?). You can think terrible thoughts about your opponent. You can spend hours reliving your previous arguments and coming up with clever new insults for your next encounter. Hey, it beats exercising or reading a book or spending time with your kids.

However, if you do decide to try to resolve the conflict—and, in the process, regain a good chunk of your free time—Lincoln can help. In fact, the excerpt on slavery can serve as a road map.

1. **Try and find something good to say about your enemy.** Bear in mind that in many cases, your enemy may be your friend (or at least used to be). What was it about this person that first drew you to them? What qualities did you used to admire in them? What admirable qualities do they still have, regardless of the fact that you're mad at them? If the enemy was never your friend, try the same exercise anyway. You probably know enough about them to pick out at least one or two good qualities.

2. **Put yourself in your enemy's place and imagine how you would react in the present situation.** This is difficult, but holds the key to resolving any conflict. Try putting yourself not only in your enemy's shoes, but inside his or her head as well. The more you can identify with someone, the less likely you are to judge or lash out at that person.

3. **Identify what you have in common with the enemy.** Aside from the current conflict, what qualities do the two of you share? Do you come from similar backgrounds? Have you gone through the same experiences?

4. **Before you say anything, pause to determine whether you're reacting or responding.** If you were in the other person's position, would what you're about to say make you more open-minded or more defensive?

Once you have done these things, you'll find yourself turning into what experts call "a reasonable person." A reasonable person is defined (at least partially) as someone who isn't perpetually angry, doesn't dwell on past disagreements, and is looking for a way to resolve conflicts. Will that win over your enemy? Maybe, maybe not (remember that several years after Lincoln participated in that debate, the Civil War still broke out). But at least it gives you a fighting chance.

CHAPTER 10

The Art of Giving Good Advice

A
S HIS CAREER PROGRESSED, LINCOLN frequently found himself dispensing advice—both solicited and unsolicited. Not surprisingly, he approached these opportunities with his characteristic grace and economy of language. Take, for instance, this short text, written in 1850 to young lawyers:

> I am not an accomplished lawyer. I find quite as much material for a lecture, in those points wherein I have failed, as in those wherein I have been moderately successful.
>
> The leading rule for the lawyer, as for the man, of every calling, is diligence. Leave nothing for tomorrow, which can be done today. Never let your correspondence fall behind.

Whatever piece of business you have in hand, before stopping, do all the labor pertaining to it which can then be done. When you bring a common-law suit, if you have the facts for doing so, write the declaration at once. If a law point be involved, examine the books, and note the authority you rely on, upon the declaration itself, where you are sure to find it when wanted. The same of defences and pleas. In business not likely to be litigated—ordinary collection cases, foreclosures, partitions, and the like—make all examinations of titles, note them, and even draft orders and decrees in advance. This course has a triple advantage; it avoids omissions and neglect, saves your labor, when once done; performs the labor out of court when you have leisure, rather than in court, when you have not.

Extemporaneous speaking should be practiced and cultivated. It is the lawyer's avenue to the public. However able and faithful he may be in other respects, people are slow to bring him business, if he cannot make a speech. And yet there is not a more fatal error to young lawyers, than relying too much on speech-making. If any one, upon his rare powers of speaking, shall claim exemption from the drudgery of the law, his case is a failure in advance.

Discourage litigation. Persuade your neighbors to

compromise whenever you can. Point out to them how the nominal winner is often a real loser—in fees, and expenses, and waste of time. As a peace-maker the lawyer has a superior opportunity of being a good man. There will still be business enough.

Never stir up litigation. A worse man can scarcely be found than one who does this. Who can be more nearly a fiend than he who habitually overhauls the Register of deeds, in search of defects in titles, whereon to stir up strife, and put money in his pocket? A moral tone ought to be infused into the profession, which should drive such men out of it.

The matter of fees is important far beyond the mere question of bread and butter involved. Properly attended to fuller justice is done to both lawyer and client. An exorbitant fee should never be claimed. As a general rule, never take your whole fee in advance, nor any more than a small retainer. When fully paid before hand, you are more than a common mortal if you can feel the same interest in the case, as if something was still in prospect for you, as well as for your client. And when you lack interest in the case, the job will very likely lack skill and diligence in the performance. Settle the amount of fee, and take a note in advance. Then you will feel that you are working for something, and you are sure to do your work *faithfully and well. Never sell a fee-note—at least, not before the consideration service is performed. It leads to negligence and dishonesty—negligence, by losing interest in the case, and dishonesty in refusing to refund, when you have allowed the consideration to fail.*

There is a vaguely popular belief that lawyers are necessarily dishonest. I say vague, because when we consider to what extent confidence, and honors are reposed in, and conferred upon lawyers by the people, it appears improbable that their impression of dishonesty is very distinct and vivid. Yet the impression, is common—almost universal. Let no young man, choosing the law for a calling, for a moment yield to this popular belief. Resolve to be honest at all events; and if, in your own judgment, you can not be an honest lawyer, resolve to be honest without being a lawyer. Choose some other occupation, rather than one in the choosing of which you do, in advance, consent to be a knave.

What makes this—one of Lincoln's most famous writings—so effective is its simplicity and honesty. It's written in a brief, casual style, foregoing the usual embellishments of a formal letter or speech. There is no lengthy preamble, no salute to the glories of law or the solemn responsibility of being a lawyer. Why not? After all, Lincoln was no stranger to such addresses; during campaigns, he frequently spoke for long periods and was often guilty of throwing in a few paragraphs of purple prose every now and then.

But what made Lincoln such a great communicator was that he never forgot who his audience was and what they wanted. He knew that the last thing a bunch of young lawyers wanted to hear was an old blowhard waxing philosophic about the glories of the law. No, they were eager and hungry for real advice that they could use—just as Lincoln had been years ago. They wanted practical, sensible pointers from someone who'd been around the block a few times. Not only would such advice help them in their careers, it would also create a favorable impression of Lincoln among them. And what better way for a budding politician to increase his profile than make a large group of potential voters very happy?

Note the quick, almost bullet-point style Lincoln employs here. Nearly every paragraph includes a "take-away" nugget that the young lawyers could easily absorb: do this, don't do that, watch out for X, beware of Y. It's a textbook example of how to give clear guidance and encouragement without being didactic or overbearing.

But it wasn't always possible to give such specific advice. Years later, as president, Lincoln found himself in a much more precarious situation: the Civil War was raging and he was in frequent contact with his field officers, who looked to him for both official and unofficial guidance. Due to the shifting nature of the war and the length of time it took to convey messages, it was often impossible for Lincoln to give step-by-step orders. Rather, he had to let them know what to do within rather wide parameters.

LETTER TO GENERAL JOHN SCHOFIELD (MAY 27, 1863)

My dear Sir:

Having relieved Gen. Curtis and assigned you to the command of the Department of the Missouri—I think it may be of some advantage for me to state to you why I did it. I did not relieve Gen. Curtis because of any full conviction that he had done wrong by commission or omission. I did it because of a conviction in my mind that the Union men of

Missouri, constituting, when united, a vast majority of the whole people, have entered into a pestilent factional quarrel among themselves, Gen. Curtis, perhaps not of choice, being the head of one faction, and Gov. Gamble that of the other. After months of labor to reconcile the difficulty, it seemed to grow worse and worse until I felt it my duty to break it up some how; and as I could not remove Gov. Gamble, I had to remove Gen. Curtis.

Now that you are in the position, I wish you to undo nothing merely because Gen. Curtis or Gov. Gamble did it; but to exercise your own judgment, and do right for the public interest. Let your military measures be strong enough to repel the invader and keep the peace, and not so strong as to unnecessarily harass and persecute the people. It is a difficult role, and so much greater will be the honor if you perform it well. If both factions, or neither, shall abuse you, you will probably be about right. Beware of being assailed by one, and praised by the other.

By this point in his administration, Lincoln knew the dangers of attempting to micromanage a volatile situation from hundreds of miles away. Such a tactic was not only doomed to failure; it would also telegraph to Lincoln's officers that he had no real faith in them to handle the situation. So rather than give Schofield ultra-specific, "do this, not that" orders, he instead made clear his trust in the general by outlining his expectations in a more oblique way. Lincoln gave Schofield a handful of principles by which to abide—a way of thinking rather than a detailed set of instructions. Schofield, when faced with a problem, could then apply those principles to the situation and know that he was acting within his bounds as a military officer, even though Lincoln was unaware of the particulars.

Again, Lincoln's letter demonstrates an acute sense of audience—he tailors the tone and content of his message for maximum impact, taking into account not only who he's talking to, but their present circumstances.

We've all known people—especially in the business world—who take the opposite approach to communication. Their cookie-cutter emails always include the same brusque attitude or sickeningly sweet greeting, regardless of who they're addressing or why. In other words, they're not really thinking about the recipient; in fact, you could even say they don't care.

The next time you find yourself dispensing advice, take a moment to think—really think—about the person on the receiving end of your wisdom. It'll have a huge impact not only on what you say, but how you say it.

Part 2:
The Professional Sphere

CHAPTER 11

Communication
Etiquette

I N RETROSPECT, IT'S PROBABLY A GOOD THING THAT
Alexander Graham Bell didn't invent the telephone until 1876. The lack of an instantaneous
means of communication over long distances (telegraph machines weren't always practical or, depending
on where you lived, even available) meant that whenever
elected U.S. leaders needed to get in touch with one
another, and they weren't within shouting distance, they
had to write letters…lots and lots of letters. Luckily for
historians, our forefathers tended to be packrats, saving
a great deal of their prodigious literary output. As a
result, libraries and museums are filled with hundreds
of thousands of pieces of correspondence from the
days of George Washington and Ben Franklin up until

the advent of modern technology, when telephones and computers edged out traditional letter writing.

Through these letters we can trace the creation of the democratic principles that led to the Constitution, the Bill of Rights, and the establishment of our fundamental governmental structure. But they also give us unprecedented insights into the personalities and characters of the people who wrote them. Abraham Lincoln is the perfect example. Spend a few days sifting through hundreds upon hundreds of his letters—both personal and political—and you can't help but feel as if you know the man. An unerring sense of decency and calm, considered judgment are present throughout his written works, which range from the days of his youth in the 1830s through the dark period of the Civil War decades later.

It's only natural to wonder how Lincoln would fare in today's fast-paced world. In this section of the book, we'll analyze his problem-solving skills and superimpose them onto the modern business environment, applying the same principles and tactics that he used to win wars (literally and figuratively) so that we can successfully deal with irritating co-workers and other everyday problems.

There's also much to be said for adopting Lincoln's nineteenth-century approach to the very act of communication—be it in an email, text message, phone call, or face-to-face meeting in the office. The rhetorical principles Lincoln employed in his speeches and letters are timeless, and just as razor-sharp today as they were in 1850. We've become so enmeshed in the new style of communication—short, fragmented messages that are frequently spoken or typed in the heat of the moment and sent across hundreds or thousands of miles in an instant—that we've forgotten the art of saying something important and saying it well.

Here are a few easy-to-use tips on organizing your thoughts and communicating in a way that will allow you to get what you want in the workplace without stirring up unnecessary arguments, hurting someone's feelings, or sabotaging your career.

1. Emphasize Clarity

One consistent quality in Lincoln's writing that is impossible to ignore is his conciseness. His letters are the written equivalent of a perfectly focused camera image—there are no fuzzy edges, no indistinct, blurry objects, and no moments of confusion. I challenge you to read even the most casual letter that Lincoln dashed off and not be able to follow along. Can you say the same for the emails and text messages you send and receive on a daily basis? You know the ones I'm talking about—where the writer types "4" instead of "for" and uses smiley-face emoticons to end every other sentence. And what about the messages that are hurriedly composed on a Blackberry while walking down a crowded street? Sometimes you feel as if you need a special decoder ring just to figure out what someone is trying to tell you.

Lincoln always knew what he wanted to accomplish in his correspondence. Each letter was written for a specific reason. He got to the point quickly. There is no meandering, no hemming and hawing, no meaningless platitudes. Even when the subject was a difficult one, he tackled it head on, usually in the first couple of sentences.

Look at the opening to this letter from January 26, 1839. Lincoln was responding to an angry letter from his associate William Butler about some local political maneuverings, in which Butler apparently accused

Lincoln of turning his back on his friends. Notice how quickly Lincoln jumped on the topic at hand, and how he made clear his strong feelings about the situation.

LETTER TO WILLIAM BUTLER
(JANUARY 26, 1839)

Dear Butler:

Your letter [of Jan. 21] is just received. You were in an ill-humor when you wrote that letter, and, no doubt, intended that I should be thrown into one also; which, however, I respectfully decline being done. All you have said about our having been bought up by Taylor, Wright, Turley, enemies &c I know you would not say, seriously, in your moments of reflection; and therefore I do not think it worth while to attempt seriously to prove the contrary to you. I only now say, that I am willing to pledge myself in black and white to cut my own throat from ear to ear, if, when I meet you, you shall seriously say, that you believe me capable of betraying my friends for any price.

The grounds of your complaint I will answer seriously. First, then, as to Athens…

Note how Lincoln established his forceful tone from

the outset; he wasn't going to take Butler's accusations lying down. He made clear he was irritated, yet he kept his cool, reiterated his innocence, and then proceeded to address the specifics of Butler's letter. Can there be any confusion about how Lincoln felt after reading that first paragraph?

When you're communicating with a colleague, the worst thing you can do is try to mask your true feelings. If you're upset about something a co-worker has said about you, let him know—and then move to correct the record. Don't spend the afternoon sulking in your cubicle. As Lincoln showed, there's a way to express displeasure without flying off the handle. He didn't lash out at Butler, but took the high road, observing somewhat wryly that his friend is in "ill-humor." And notice that after he "stakes his claim" and professed his innocence, he didn't linger on the subject. He quickly moved on to answer the specifics of Butler's complaints against him and explain the situation in great detail.

2. Be Prepared

But what if you're not sure what you want (or need) to say? You don't have clarity because you don't know what type of message you should send. Perhaps you've received an email that requires a response, but you're having trouble coming up with a coherent reply. It happens all the time, especially if your boss asks for your thoughts on a thorny business issue, or a client calls up out of the blue and asks for advice on a complicated problem.

Oftentimes we feel the need to respond immediately. An email pops up in our inbox and sits there, flashing, waiting for a reply. *The clock is ticking*, we think. *If I don't respond right away, they'll think I'm goofing off or watching YouTube instead of working.* It's as if we're on one of those high-pressure quiz shows where you have ten seconds to answer a trivia question, and if you wait too long, you miss the chance to win a million dollars. We are told over and over again that we live in a fast-paced world where business competition is fierce and speed is oftentimes a more valuable commodity than money. The company that can provide answers more quickly than their competitors can come out on top.

All of this is true. Yes, quick turnaround times are important—but only if the end product is of sufficient quality to satisfy the person who asks for it. In other words, if a client wants a new computer delivered in twenty-four hours, and you send it to him, but the hard drive isn't fully assembled, the CD-ROM drive isn't attached properly, and the monitor has a big crack in the screen, will that customer be satisfied? Of course not! Yes, technically, you delivered a computer to him in twenty-four hours, but it was a piece of crap. You met the deadline, but the end product wasn't worth the price of the overnight delivery.

The same is true with communication. If your boss sends you an email about a problem and asks, "What do you think?" he or she probably would like an answer immediately. And he or she would probably also like to find a way to lose thirty pounds in one day, or to make a million dollars overnight. It's natural to want an instant response, to seek instant gratification. But often it's just not practical.

Human beings aren't walking vending machines. We don't dispense advice or solutions immediately after someone expresses a need—and people who do tend to give very bad advice. Sometimes a proper response just takes time. So when your boss sends you an email at nine o'clock in the morning stating, "What the hell are we going to do about the Johnson account?" or "Bob just called in sick, and Carol is on maternity leave, we need to figure out how we're going to finish our presentation on time," you can shoot back an email stating, "I'm on it. Let's meet this afternoon to discuss our options. How's 2:00 p.m.?" Or you can reply with: "This is a serious situation, no doubt about it. I've cleared my desk and plan on spending the entire morning exploring our options and preparing some solid alternatives. I'll send you an email summarizing my findings no later than 2:00 p.m." That way, you've given yourself some breathing room, allowed time for yourself to gather your thoughts and deliver a response that actually looks as if it was thought up by an adult.

3. Write the Nineteenth-Century Way

Of course, Lincoln and his contemporaries didn't have to worry about rapid response. In his day, the entire country moved at a snail's pace compared to today's 24-7 global logistics network. If you received a letter on a Tuesday, it didn't really matter if you replied right away or waited a day or so; it was still going to take several days, and probably much longer, for your reply to reach its destination via the local mail train or perhaps even by horseback. Except in the direst of circumstances, no one expected an immediate response to their letters.

With no imaginary stopwatch ticking away above their heads, correspondents were able to take their time and actually think about what they wanted to say. What a concept! Lincoln always chose his words carefully. You get the sense that he had thought long and hard about not only what he wanted to say, but how he wanted to say it and in what order—the organization is just as important as the content.

There was another reason why Lincoln was careful about the words he put on paper: the stakes were much higher than they are in today's wired world. As president, Lincoln often communicated about subjects that were vital to the security and prosperity of an entire nation, never more so than during the Civil War. There was no room for error or ambiguity. He had to make sure the commanding officer in the field understood exactly what he was telling them to do, and exactly where he stood on a particular political or military issue. If Lincoln failed to make his position clearly known, the results could be disastrous. And it wasn't as if the recipient could simply whip out a cell phone, call him up, and say, "Hey Abe, in that third paragraph, did you mean 'civil war' or 'silly war'? I can't really tell."

This is why leaders of the era put such an enormous premium on writing skills. There were no do-overs. Their approach wasn't "I need to respond right away," but "I need to get this right the first time—or else." Try putting yourself in a similar frame of mind when the time comes to write an important memo or email. Of course, you shouldn't act as if the weight of the free world is resting on your shoulders, but you should put a premium on clarity. Are your words and statements clear and direct? Is there any room for ambiguity or misinterpretation? Could a reasonable person read what you've written and come away with a different idea than the one you intended? Try to poke holes in your sentences. Test your words and make sure they hold up to scrutiny.

In a business environment, the worst response you can get to an email isn't "No," or "You're an idiot."

The worst response is a simple, "Huh?" If your boss asks for your opinion, make sure he doesn't need an interpreter to figure out what you mean. Wasting time is a much more impeachable offense than spending a few hours crafting a well-thought response.

4. Never Be Spontaneous

Think back to the last time you saw an amazing live performance. Maybe you attended a classical music concert, caught a Broadway musical, or saw the Rolling Stones on their umpteenth world tour. Regardless, the music was top-notch, the performers knocked it out of the park, and the entire production rolled along like a well-oiled machine. You walked away a satisfied customer. But while you were enjoying the show, did you think of the months of rehearsal it took to deliver such a flawless product? Probably not; you most likely took it for granted that a lot of preparation must have been involved. After all, it's not as if the performers just showed up one night, decided to put on a show, and happened to nail it perfectly the first time.

We have to look at important business communications in the same way. Lincoln's letters are textbook examples of grace and economy, but it would be wrong to assume that he got them right the first time—that what we see on the page is the first and only draft. Like any fine performance, musical or rhetorical, it's certain that Lincoln went through several iterations of his most important letters, honing his message, making sure the tone and content was exactly what he wanted to convey. The finished product is elegant and polished, but it didn't start out that way.

An ancient parable illustrates the necessity of practice and forethought. The emperor's wife had recently died, and he commissioned one of the country's most celebrated artists to paint her portrait. He frequently sent his guards to check on his progress, but each time they inquired, the artist replied, "Not yet, not yet." Finally, after months of waiting, the emperor himself arrived at the artist's house with his guards. He demanded that the artist paint his wife's portrait at once, or else he would order the guards to kill him. The artist sighed, picked up his brush, and with what seemed almost no effort at all, proceeded to paint an astonishing likeness of the emperor's late wife. When he finished, the emperor was baffled.

"Why did you make me wait so long and risk losing your life when you could have painted such a masterpiece at any time?" he asked.

The artist merely shook his head and said, "I could not have painted it before today." He then gestured to a closed door, and the emperor opened it. There, inside a small room that was obviously the artist's studio, the walls were covered with hundreds of sketches and watercolors of the emperor's wife: detailed renderings of her eyes, ears, nose, and virtually every other aspect of her appearance. The emperor realized that the artist had been working day and night for months in order to be able to paint the portrait with such apparent ease. He bowed to the artist and accepted the painting gratefully.

Now, this doesn't mean you should treat each email you write as if it were a literary treasure, nor should you labor for three hours over the precise wording of a reply when someone asks if you want to grab a sandwich for lunch. But as Lincoln's own letters show, banishing that imaginary countdown clock from your head and taking the time to get your thoughts in order will not only make you look better, it can also help you avoid the consequences of reacting emotionally: hurt feelings, bruised egos, or even a reprimand from your boss. Not to mention the fact that if you start lashing out at the people you work with, chances are it will affect the performance of the entire office.

So what should you do the next time you receive an important email and you're not sure how to respond? Resolve from the outset that you will write at least one rough draft of your reply before clicking the "send" button.

There's no secret, one-size-fits-all formula to organizing your thoughts. Every person and situation is different. But writing a draft with the knowledge that no one else will see it allows you to free up your mind and brainstorm about what you really want to say and how you want to say it. If you're angry or stressed, those emotions will come out on the page; if you're being honest, you won't be able to hide them. And that's exactly what you want: to get all of the dirty laundry on the table so that you can start discarding the stuff that doesn't belong. Angry words will almost jump out at you from the computer screen. Find them, isolate them, and cut them. If they keep cropping up, write an email to yourself and vent all of your frustrations. Get the name-calling and blame-putting out of your system. Once it's finished, delete the email and get back to the task at hand.

Clearing your writing of negative emotions is like pulling weeds in a garden. It can be hard work, but if you want the good stuff to grow, you have to do it. And once the weeds are out of the way, the flowers are so much easier to see! Likewise, when you cut out the anger, stress, and fear from your writing, the reader is able to see the reason, logic, and facts. If you have something important to say, don't let emotional language obscure it.

5. Be Judicious with Your Communication

Have you ever wondered what would happen if, by some absurd twist of fate, the government passed a drastic law limiting the number of emails you could send to, say, five a day? It could never happen, of course, but let's pretend for a moment. What would you do?

Obviously, you'd have to think very, very carefully before you sent an email—no more "Hey, what's up?"

messages, no "Hey, did you see X Television Show last night?" It would be a huge adjustment, and a lot of us would probably start having withdrawal symptoms. We've become accustomed to being able to communicate whenever and wherever we want for as long as we want. Most phone companies offer free text messaging or charge only a nominal fee. Your Internet provider charges you the same amount each month, regardless of whether you send ten emails or ten thousand. And each email can be a couple of sentences long or twelve pages—it doesn't matter.

This has led to a phenomenon I call "keyboard diarrhea." Because there's no real limit or penalty on the volume of electronic messages we can send, we go for broke, sending hundreds of messages each week, a never-ending stream of data pumped out in a variety of different formats. We email, text, Twitter, and blog about any thought that pops into our heads— and sometimes we don't even wait until we have a thought. Communication has never been this easy or accessible in the entire history of mankind. We're probably just a few years away from having circuits implanted in our brains to allow us to make phone calls simply by opening our mouths and clicking our tongues.

In one respect, this is fantastic; the technological changes of the past twenty years have revolutionized global business and culture in ways too numerous to mention. But there's a huge downside, too. Slowly but surely, generation by generation, we're forgetting the real art of communication: how to construct an argument, how to gather one's thoughts into coherent sentences and paragraphs. Instead, we fire short bursts of highly compressed, half-formed thoughts back and forth on our cell phones and computers. An entirely new language has been created solely for text messaging, replete with abbreviations and shortcuts that slice and dice the English language into nano-sized chunks.

Lincoln and his contemporaries, of course, lived in a very different environment. The most common method of communication—letter writing—was a long and laborious process: dipping a quill in an inkwell and scratching out a few words before it ran dry, then repeating the process over and over again. One didn't sit down and casually dash off a few dozen letters and memos every day; there simply wasn't time. And if you happened to live in a rural area, chances are the nearest "office supply store" (most likely a dry goods dealer or general store) was several miles away by horseback, if you were lucky. That meant you had to ration your use of ink and paper so that you didn't run out.

As a result of these limitations, people had to think long and hard about what they wanted to say before they started writing. Rambling simply wasn't an option. Because the act of writing letters was so elaborate, they were seen as important, not a casual means of passing the time or chatting with distant friends and relatives.

In the twentieth century, technological advances made letter writing much easier. The ballpoint pen and typewriter became the instant messages of their day, allowing people to write more letters and communicate much more quickly (and about more frivolous subjects) than ever before. The pace kept quickening with the advent of cheap and reliable telephone service and, finally, the Internet, which brings us to our present glut of communication.

So what does all of this have to do with office email? Plenty. Co-workers bombard each other—and their bosses—with irrelevant or borderline-unnecessary email messages every day. We've all had the experience of leaving for an afternoon meeting and returning a few hours later to find our inbox filled with three dozen new messages, many of them multiple emails from the same person who's adding on to their original thought with corrections or a string of "P.S." add-ons. What fun! Or perhaps we find ourselves answering emails ten seconds after we read them, without really thinking through our response; it's as if we're trying to see who can hit the "reply" button first.

If you want to improve the way you communicate in the workplace, try adopting a nineteenth-century attitude. Approach each email the way our forebears approached writing a letter. Just because you can fire off a message in ten seconds doesn't mean you should. Be judicious with your email. Take the time to organize your thoughts and bundle several short messages into a single email. The recipient will appreciate it, and who knows? Your efficiency may even rub off on them, resulting in clearer emails...and fewer of them!

CHAPTER 12

Leadership and Management under Fire

OR SEASONED BUSINESS VETERANS AS WELL as those just starting out in their careers, Lincoln's letters written during the Civil War constitute a veritable encyclopedia on how to lead a large group of people and manage them under extremely difficult circumstances. In this chapter, we'll look at several examples of Lincoln's grace under fire and, more importantly, how you can lead like Lincoln did when everything seems to be going wrong.

Reading Lincoln's war-era correspondence is a surprising exercise in several respects. For one thing, you realize how much time and energy he expended dealing with the hurt feelings and bruised egos of his commanding officers in the field. Lincoln proved to be a master at the art of assuaging his generals' often volatile emotions and managing his far-flung officer corps with astounding deftness. The lessons for today's managers are obvious: managing your twenty-first-century team—with its rainbow of personality types, backgrounds, and ambitions—with skill and grace is both difficult and crucial for succeeding in the increasingly competitive global marketplace.

Hearts and Minds

In this letter, a response to what we can only assume was a rather despairing dispatch, Lincoln attempted to bolster the confidence of Major General Joseph Hooker, who had suffered a stinging defeat in Chancellorsville, Virginia, at the hands of Confederate general Robert E. Lee a few weeks earlier. At this point, Lincoln's confidence in Hooker was waning, and just days after he received the letter, Hooker would in fact offer his resignation. However, though he may even have sensed that the end was near, Lincoln nevertheless dealt with Hooker in a frank and dignified manner.

Letter to General Joseph Hooker (June 16, 1863)

My dear General:

I send you this by the hand of Captain Dahlgren. Your dispatch of 11:30 a.m. to-day is just received. When you say I have long been aware that you do not enjoy the confidence of the major-general commanding, you state the case much too strongly.

You do not lack his confidence in any degree to do you any harm. On seeing him, after telegraphing you this morning, I found him more nearly agreeing with you than I was myself. Surely you do not mean to understand that I am withholding my confidence from you when I happen to express an opinion (certainly never discourteously) differing from one of your own.

I believe Halleck is dissatisfied with you to this extent only, that he knows that you write and telegraph ("report," as he calls it) to me. I think he is wrong to find fault with this; but I do not think he withholds any support from you on account of it. If you and he would use the same frankness to one another, and to me, that I use to both of you, there would be no diffi-culty. I need and must have the professional skill of both, and yet these suspicions tend to deprive me of both.

I believe you are aware that since you took command of the army I have not believed you had any chance to effect anything till now. As it looks to me, Lee's now returning toward Harper's Ferry gives you back the chance that I thought McClellan lost last fall. Quite possibly I was wrong both then and now; but, in the great responsibility resting upon me, I cannot be entirely silent. Now, all I ask is that you will be in such mood that we can get into our action the best cordial judgment of yourself and General Halleck, with my poor mite added, if indeed he and you shall think it entitled to any consideration at all.

Note how Lincoln refused to sugarcoat the situation and deny reality simply to boost Hooker's spirits momentarily. There are no "Hey, you're doing great!" or "Everyone is saying wonderful things about you" sentiments. This rhetorical decision shouldn't be underestimated. It's only speculation, of course, but the temptation to whitewash the situation was probably considerable. After all, Lincoln knew the stress Hooker was under, and another clash with Lee's forces was inevitable. Why not shade the truth, pretend everything was rosy, and buck up his ego to get through the next few weeks?

And yet Lincoln dealt with the situation head-on, with no false promises or empty compliments. He acknowledged that Hooker's commanding officer was dissatisfied, though not to the extent Hooker imagined. He then gently attempted to nudge Hooker back into line, pointing out the absurdity of assuming Lincoln had lost confidence in him every time they disagreed on battlefield strategy. Then the kicker: "If you and he would use the same frankness to one another, and to me, that I use to both of you, there would be no difficulty. I need and must have the professional skill of both, and yet these suspicions tend to deprive me of both." It's an elegant yet forceful scolding—strong enough to get Hooker's attention, but written in such a way that it wouldn't embarrass or anger him. There is no anger in Lincoln's words, just blunt truthfulness. His goal was not to vent his own frustrations—he probably did that in private—but to attempt to improve Hooker's worrisome performance and mind-set.

However, Lincoln was quick to give praise when it was justified. The following letter from 1861 is a classic example of how to encourage an employee who has performed admirably, and at great personal sacrifice:

LETTER TO
BRIGADIER GENERAL JOHN MCCLERNAND
(NOV. 10, 1861)

My Dear Sir

This is not an official but a social letter. You have had a battle, and without being able to judge as to the precise measure of its value, I think it is safe to say that you, and all with you have done honor to yourselves and the flag and service to the country. Most gratefully do I thank you and them. In my present position, I must care for the whole nation; but I hope it will be no injustice to any other state, for me to indulge in a little home pride, that Illinois does not disappoint us.

I have just closed a long interview with Mr. Washburne in which he has detailed the many difficulties you, and those with you labor under. Be assured, we do not forget or neglect you. Much, very much, goes undone: but it is because we have not the power to do it faster than we do. Some of your forces are without arms, but the same is true here, and at every other place where we have considerable bodies of troops. The plain matter-of-fact is, our good people have rushed to the rescue of the Government, faster than the government can find arms to put into their hands.

> *It would be agreeable to each division of the army to know its own precise destination: but the Government cannot immediately, nor inflexibly at any time, determine as to all; nor if determined, can it tell its friends without at the same time telling its enemies.*
>
> *We know you do all as wisely and well as you can; and you will not be deceived if you conclude the same is true of us. Please give my respects and thanks to all.*

How could you not feel better after receiving such a letter from your boss? Again, note the evenness of Lincoln's tone here. He didn't gush or pour on the compliments too thickly. He was, first and foremost, genuine. It's clear that he meant every word he wrote, and his end goal—to encourage an officer who has witnessed the worst horrors of the battlefield—is reflected in nearly every line. Notice also how Lincoln acknowledged McClernand's concerns about the flow of information and materiel near the end of the letter and explained the reality of the situation without becoming argumentative or defensive.

Urgency

During the war, Lincoln frequently found it necessary to write letters of immense urgency. A man of
lesser experience might have fallen into the trap of
becoming overly emotional, but by this point in his
career, Lincoln had developed an enviable control
over tone and language; he was able to communicate
intense emotions without appearing panicked or out of
control. In today's hyper-accelerated workplace, where
deadlines loom around every office corner, we would
do well to study Lincoln's approach.

Let's look at the following letter to General Don
Buell. Lincoln was at odds with his officer over battlefield strategy, and was also becoming increasingly
concerned about the personal safety of Union allies in
Tennessee. This is, literally, a life-and-death situation:

LETTER TO
BRIGADIER GENERAL DON C. BUELL
(JANUARY 6, 1862)

My dear Sir,
Your dispatch of yesterday has been received, and it
disappoints me and distresses me. I have shown it to Gen.

McClellan, who says he will write you to-day. I am not competent to criticize your views; and therefore what I offer is merely in justification of myself. Of the two, I would rather have a point on the Railroad south of Cumberland Gap, than Nashville, first, because it cuts a great artery of the enemies' communication, which Nashville does not, and secondly because it is in the midst of loyal people, who would rally around it, while Nashville is not. Again, I cannot see why the movement on East Tennessee would not be a diversion in your favor, rather than a disadvantage, assuming that a movement towards Nashville is the main object.

But my distress is that our friends in East Tennessee are being hanged and driven to despair, and even now I fear, are thinking of taking rebel arms for the sake of personal protection. In this we lose the most valuable stake we have in the South. My dispatch, to which yours is an answer, was sent with the knowledge of Senator Johnson and Representative Maynard of East Tennessee, and they will be upon me to know the answer, which I cannot safely show them. They would despair—possibly resign to go and save their families somehow, or die with them.

I do not intend this to be an order in any sense, but merely, as intimated before, to show you the grounds of my anxiety.

Lincoln managed to communicate the extreme urgency of the situation without engaging in unnecessary hyperbole. Note the structure of this brief letter. He began by cutting straight to the chase: "Your dispatch of yesterday has been received, and it disappoints and distresses me." How many times have we seen Lincoln start a letter with a similar statement? Not only does such an opening immediately grab his reader's attention, it also put Lincoln immediately on the offensive. He was the one who set the tone, and in this case, it's one of the utmost seriousness.

After plainly—but not emotionally—stating his feelings, Lincoln then explained, in clear and simple language, his preferred strategy. He made his case not by tearing down Buell's views, but by elucidating his own. He was not afraid to explain himself, and was confident that his strategy could withstand Buell's expert criticism.

And then, in the penultimate paragraph, he moved from a logical argument to an emotional one. The shift is intentionally abrupt: "our friends in East Tennessee are being hanged and driven to despair." Lincoln

wanted to impress upon Buell the urgency of the moment. Even today, his words are chilling.

Deciding when to call upon your readers' emotions and essentially shock them into action can be tricky. It's a card that should be played rarely. Much of the power of this letter stems from the fact that Lincoln was not someone who engaged in such rhetoric on a regular basis. If Buell was used to reading such sentiments in Lincoln's correspondence, the effect would have been much different.

Sweating the Small Stuff

Another way in which Lincoln demonstrated excellent leadership was his ability to engage his subordinates in respectful debate and intelligently discuss the problems they faced. By demonstrating a mastery of the nitty-gritty details, he increased their confidence in him—here was a leader who truly understood their day-to-day worries and was as engaged with battlefield strategy as they were, even though he was hundreds of miles away.

In high school algebra class, you may recall being required to "show your work"—to demonstrate the step-by-step process you used to arrive at the solution for an equation. It wasn't enough to simply say "X = 12." You had to show how you figured it out. The same principle applies in managing people. Rather than just deliver orders with no explanation, it's often extremely helpful to spend some time explaining to your employees why you've decided to go with Plan A rather than Plan B, so that they understand your reasoning and the potential benefit to the company. This doesn't mean you have to defend every decision and justify the slightest moves to your team, but when the stakes are high, letting them know that you understand all sides of the problem—and perhaps even showing off a little by demonstrating your grasp of the situation—can calm their anxieties.

LETTER TO
BRIGADIER GENERAL DON C. BUELL
(JANUARY 13, 1862)

My dear Sir:
Your dispatch of yesterday is received, in which you say "I have received your letter and Gen. McClellan's; and will, at once devote all my efforts to your views, and his." In the

midst of my many cares, I have not seen, or asked to see, Gen. McClellan's letter to you. For my own views, I have not offered, and do not now offer them as orders; and while I am glad to have them respectfully considered, I would blame you to follow them contrary to your own clear judgment—unless I should put them in the form of orders. As to Gen. McClellan's views, you understand your duty in regard to them better than I do.

With this preliminary, I state my general idea of this war to be that we have the greater numbers, and the enemy has the greater facility of concentrating forces upon points of collision; that we must fail, unless we can find some way of making our advantage an over-match for his; and that this can only be done by menacing him with superior forces at different points, at the same time; so that we can safely attack, one, or both, if he makes no change; and if he weakens one to strengthen the other, forbear to attack the strengthened one, but seize, and hold the weakened one, gaining so much.

To illustrate, suppose last summer, when Winchester ran away to reinforce Manassas, we had forborne to attack Manassas, but had seized and held Winchester. I mention this to illustrate, and not to criticize. I did not lose confidence in McDowell, and I think less harshly of Patterson than some others seem to. In application of the general rule I am suggesting, every particular case will have its modifying circumstances, among which the most constantly present, and most difficult to meet, will be the want of perfect knowledge of the enemies' movements. This had its part in the Bull–Run case; but worse, in that case, was the expiration of the terms of the three months men.

Applying the principle to your case, my idea is that Halleck shall menace Columbus, and "down river" generally; while you menace Bowling Green, and East Tennessee. If the enemy shall concentrate at Bowling Green, do not retire from his front; yet do not fight him there, either, but seize Columbus and East Tennessee, one or both, left exposed by the concentration at Bowling Green. It is matter of no small anxiety to me and one which I am sure you will not overlook, that the East Tennessee line, is so long, and over so bad a road.

This letter should hang in every manager's office. The next time you find yourself struggling to gather your thoughts and deliver a clear set of instructions to your employees, read Lincoln's masterful blend of advice ("I would blame you to follow them contrary to your own clear judgment") and strategic wisdom.

Notice how, in the second paragraph, he laid out in full what might be termed his "philosophy of battle," then immediately followed up those rather abstract thoughts with a concrete example to drive home the point.

Also, imagine for a moment how General Buell felt after reading this letter. Again, not to overstate the matter, but maintaining his officers' trust and confidence was of paramount importance to Lincoln. He knew that they were facing inhuman amounts of stress on a daily basis, while he sat safely ensconced in the White House; his communications to them had to be pitch-perfect, or else he would come off sounding like a distant and uninterested ruler. Do you imagine that Buell was encouraged after reading Lincoln's letter? Was his confidence in the commander in chief increased or diminished? Even if he disagreed with the strategy Lincoln laid out, there was no question as to what the president actually thought and what he expected of Buell.

Dropping the Hammer

Another problem Lincoln faced during the war was how to reject terrible ideas from his commanding officers without destroying their morale. As we have seen, the correspondence between Lincoln and his military leaders flowed thick and fast; he was engaged in the day-to-day planning of the war in a way that is hard to comprehend today. But this open line of communication between the battlefield and the White House had its drawbacks, too. Lincoln was barraged with questions, challenges to his own orders, and lame-brained strategies. Everyone had an opinion, and everyone, it seems, wrote Lincoln a letter telling him about it.

Business executives face the same dilemma. A healthy company is one that encourages employees to offer suggestions and ideas for improvement and growth. But what happens when the ideas stink? How do you reject the idea without rejecting the person?

Lincoln had to navigate such a minefield in the waning months of 1862, when one of his generals, Nathaniel Banks, came up with an unwieldy and costly idea. Here, an obviously frustrated Lincoln reprimands the officer for attempting to embark on a boondoggle of epic proportions.

LETTER TO GENERAL NATHANIEL BANKS
(NOV. 22, 1862)

My dear General Banks

Early last week you left me in high hope with your assurance that you would be off with your expedition at the end of that week, or early in this. It is now the end of this, and I have just been overwhelmed and confounded with the sight of a requisition made by you, which, I am assured, can not be filled, and got off within an hour short of two months! I inclose you a copy of the requisition, in some hope that it is not genuine—that you have never seen it.

My dear General, this expanding, and piling up of impedimenta, has been, so far, almost our ruin, and will be our final ruin if it is not abandoned. If you had the articles of this requisition upon the wharf, with the necessary animals to make them of any use, and forage for the animals, you could not get vessels together in two weeks to carry the whole, to say nothing of your twenty thousand men; and, having the vessels, you could not put the cargoes aboard in two weeks more. And, after all, where you are going, you have no use for them. When you parted with me, you had no such idea in your mind. I know you had not, or you could not have expected to be off so soon as you said. You must get back to something like the plan you had then, or your expedition is a failure before you start. You must be off before Congress meets. You would be better off any where, and especially where you are going, for not having a thousand wagons, doing nothing but hauling forage to feed the animals that draw them, and taking at least two thousand men to care for the wagons and animals, who otherwise might be two thousand good soldiers.

Now dear General, do not think this is an ill-natured letter—it is the very reverse. The simple publication of this requisition would ruin you.

Lincoln didn't hide his displeasure, but he softened the blow by framing his rejection as a way of saving Banks's career. He was, in effect, trying to rescue Banks from the consequences of his bad idea ("The simple publication of this requisition would ruin you").

But it wasn't enough to simply reject Banks's plan. Lincoln again "showed his work" and explained his reasoning. Banks probably wasn't happy when he read the letter, but Lincoln's logical explanation no doubt made it easier to accept the decision.

There is seemingly no end to the types of problems a successful executive encounters in the workplace on a daily basis. But as we have seen from these examples, clear communication and a willingness to explain one's decisions can go a long way toward keeping your business ship headed in the right direction—and making sure your crew doesn't mutiny!

CHAPTER 13

Settling a Disagreement in the Workplace

S OME THINGS NEVER CHANGE. TAKE EMPLOYEES, for instance: You can always count on at least one of them to disagree with the boss's decision. Maybe you're a supervisor who's facing unrest among the ranks. During the Civil War, Lincoln certainly had his share of detractors in the military. Oftentimes, the generals under his direct command disagreed with his strategic decisions. Can you imagine the pressure? Lincoln was trying to win a war between the states—a war that would determine the future of the country—and his own officers questioned his judgment. And yet, as we've seen time and again, Lincoln refused to take the easy road. He refused to lash out at his generals or give them the Donald Trump "my way or the highway" ultimatum.

And for good reason. He was in a war, after all, and good, experienced generals were hard to come by. If he started firing everyone who disagreed with him, morale among the other officers—not to mention the enlisted troops—would have plummeted.

In the following excerpt, Lincoln addressed General George McClellan, who disagreed with Lincoln over the Union army's next move.

LETTER TO GENERAL McCLELLAN (FEBRUARY 3, 1862)

My dear Sir,

You and I have distinct, and different plans for a movement of the Army of the Potomac—yours to be down the Chesapeake, up the Rappahannock to Urbana and across land to the terminus of the railroad on the York River—; mine to move directly to a point on the railroad southwest of Manassas.

If you will give me satisfactory answers to the following questions, I shall gladly yield my plan to yours.

1st. Does not your plan involve a greatly larger expenditure of time and money than mine?

2nd. Wherein is a victory more certain by your plan than mine?

3rd. Wherein is a victory more valuable by your plan than mine?

4th. In fact, would it not be less valuable in this, that it would break no great line of the enemy's communications, while mine would?

5th. In case of disaster, would not a retreat be more difficult by your plan than mine?

Lincoln showed a willingness to listen to his employee. At the very beginning of the letter, Lincoln framed the situation: "You and I have distinct and different plans for a movement of the Army of the Potomac." He then did what few bosses would have the guts to do: agreed to go along with his employee's plan, provided that McClellan could come up with a strong argument for it. This wasn't a trick or ploy on Lincoln's part; he didn't set up an impossible test for McClellan to try and inevitably fail. He simply asked a series of tough but fair questions.

Note, too, how Lincoln didn't lash out at McClellan for daring to disagree with the president of the United States. He treated the general—his subordinate—with respect.

The office is often a tense place, and sometimes it is tempting for supervisors to simply bark out orders and not worry about the consequences. But Lincoln was wise enough to realize the stakes of this particular situation. The truth is, some employees are more important than others, especially during crises when specialized knowledge and skills are needed. Some employees need to be treated as if they are partners rather than subordinates.

Most importantly, Lincoln realized this wasn't about his ego. He could have easily told McClellan to stop whining and follow his orders. That would have given the president a quick burst of satisfaction, but nothing more. And it could have had disastrous consequences later. Lincoln was by no means a perfect wartime leader, but he rarely lost sight of the big picture.

CHAPTER 14

Acknowledging a Mistake

WHAT'S WORSE THAN HAVING TO ADMIT YOU made a mistake? Having to admit it to an employee. Lincoln had to swallow his pride on occasion, just like everyone does—but he taught us how to do it with style and grace. Check out this brief letter he wrote to General Ulysses S. Grant:

LETTER TO GENERAL GRANT
(JULY 13, 1863)

My dear General,

I do not remember that you and I ever met personally. I write this now as a grateful acknowledgment for the almost inesti-mable service you have done the country. I wish to say a word further. When you first reached the vicinity of Vicksburg, I thought you should do what you finally did—march the troops across the neck, run the batteries with the transports, and thus go below; and I never had any faith, except a general hope that you knew better than I, that the Yazoo Pass expedition and the like could succeed. When you got below and took Port Gibson, Grand Gulf, and vicinity, I thought you should go down the river and join General Banks, and when you turned northward, east of the Big Black, I feared it was a mistake. I now wish to make the personal acknowledgment that you were right and I was wrong.

Yours very truly,

A. Lincoln

The seven bravest, most courageous words a boss can say to an employee—or one person can say to another person, for that matter—are, "You were right and I was wrong." Can anyone doubt that Grant's loyalty to Lincoln grew after receiving this brief but heartfelt letter? Lincoln's admission was not only an act of humility; it was also a sign of his respect for his general.

Note how Lincoln kept the letter short and to the point. He did not try to gloss over the fact that he at one time doubted Grant's judgment, nor did he attempt to defend his previous opinions; the tone is not defensive, but plainly honest. Sound familiar? We've seen Lincoln use this technique over and over again; the more important the message he needed to communicate, the fewer superfluous words he used.

One might ask why Lincoln decided to admit his lack of faith in Grant's decision in the first place. After all, it wasn't as if Lincoln had publicly declared that Grant was screwing things up; if he had, then an apology would certainly be in order. But from what we can tell, Lincoln had kept his reservations to himself. Why, then, admit that he was wrong, if no one would ever know? Only Lincoln knew for sure, but it seems obvious that he wanted to encourage Grant.

Note, too, that Lincoln didn't write such letters willy-nilly. He didn't go around constantly apologizing to his military officers every time he secretly questioned their decisions. Had he done so, his authority and reputation would have been severely diminished. Acknowledging his mistake to a subordinate was a rare event—and that's what made it so powerful.

CHAPTER 15

Reprimanding Employees

O NE OF THE MOST UNCOMFORTABLE TASKS A supervisor has is reprimanding employees. No one enjoys it—at least, no one *should* enjoy it (we'll leave sadistic bosses out of the equation for the moment). Admonishing an employee for unacceptable behavior while at the same time keeping that person a happy and productive member of your team is a difficult and delicate balancing act.

Lincoln had plenty of experience reprimanding various military officers during the Civil War—and luckily for us, much of that correspondence has survived. We can learn a lot about the way he handled disagreements (and worse) under very tense and trying circumstances.

LETTER TO MOULTON
(JULY 31, 1863)

My dear Sir,

There has been a good deal of complaint against you by your superior officers of the Provost-Marshal-General's Department, and your removal has been strongly urged on the ground of "persistent disobedience of orders and neglect of duty."

Firmly convinced, as I am, of the patriotism of your motives, I am unwilling to do anything in your case which may seem unnecessarily harsh or at variance with the feelings of personal respect and esteem with which I have always regarded you. I consider your services in your district valuable, and should be sorry to lose them. It is unnecessary for me to state, however, that when differences of opinion arise between officers of the government, the ranking officer must be obeyed. You of course recognize as clearly as I do the importance of this rule.

I hope you will conclude to go on in your present position under the regulations of the department. I wish you would write to me.

Here, Lincoln employed a skillful bit of rhetorical strategy to deal with a recalcitrant junior officer. From the outset, he framed the situation as, "They want me to get rid of you, but I'm going to give you one more chance." In other words, Lincoln portrayed himself as Moulton's last, best hope—not just another superior officer looking for a reason to criticize him. He also appealed to Moulton's ego ("Firmly convinced, as I am, of the patriotism of your motives…"). No doubt, Moulton felt he was doing the right thing by disobeying his superiors' orders; Lincoln found a clever way to agree with him, sort of, by praising his motives but criticizing his actions. And having done so, he lowered the hammer: "the ranking officer must be obeyed."

Note, too, how Lincoln got right to the point—no wasted words or energy. With the very first line of the letter, he stated the situation and then was off to the races. We see the same technique employed in the following letter to Major General Hunter.

Letter to Major General Hunter (Dec. 31, 1861)

Dear Sir,

Yours of the 23rd. is received, and I am constrained to say it is difficult to answer so ugly a letter in good temper. I am, as you intimate, losing much of the great confidence I placed in you, not from any act or omission of yours touching the public service, up to the time you were sent to Leavenworth, but from the flood of grumbling despatches and letters I have seen from you since.

I knew you were being ordered to Leavenworth at the time it was done; and I aver that with as tender a regard for your honor and your sensibilities as I had for my own, it never occurred to me that you were being "humiliated, insulted, and disgraced"; nor have I, up to this day, heard an intimation that you have been wronged, coming from any one but yourself. No one has blamed you for the retrograde movement from Springfield, nor for the information you gave General Cameron; and this you could readily understand, if it were not for your unwarranted assumption that the ordering you to Leavenworth must necessarily have been done as a punishment for some fault.

I thought then, and think yet, the position assigned to you is as responsible, and as honorable, as that assigned to Buell—I know that General McClellan expected more important results from it. My impression is that at the time you were assigned to the new Western Department, it had not been determined to replace General Sherman in Kentucky; but of this I am not certain, because the idea that a command in Kentucky was very desirable, and one in the farther West undesirable, had never occurred to me.

You constantly speak of being placed in command of only 3,000. Now, tell me, is this not mere impatience? Have you not known all the while that you are to command four or five times that many. I have been, and am sincerely your friend; and if, as such, I dare to make a suggestion, I would say you are adopting the best possible way to ruin yourself. "Act well your part, there all the honor lies." He who does something at the head of one regiment, will eclipse him who does nothing at the head of a hundred.

Your friend, as ever,

A. Lincoln

Lincoln's stylistic approach in this letter is arresting; he was grim and brutally frank. Because he was dealing with a high-ranking officer, he could adopt a more personal tone than if he were corresponding with a junior officer. But even this "personal touch" might have been a deliberate strategy to catch Major General Hunter off guard, or at the very least a technique meant to drive home the serious nature of Lincoln's disagreement. The president didn't lose his temper, but it was clear that he was more than a little irritated with Hunter.

In the previous letter to Moulton, Lincoln sought to sooth ruffled feathers and restore a bruised ego; but his intent in this letter is quite different. There are no lighthearted quips or attempts at humor; Lincoln wasn't trying to make Hunter feel better about himself. In short, Lincoln's tone fits the subject matter of his letter. A serious problem requires a serious approach.

We've all worked with people who have misapplied this principle: the boss who was responsible for a $20 million account, but flew into a rage whenever someone used too many office supplies; the supervisor who turned a blind eye to major problems with an employee or important project, but spent hours picking out new drapes for the conference room; the co-worker who took even the slightest criticism personally and burst into tears. Imbalance is everywhere; it can permeate an entire company. It takes discipline and thoughtfulness to make sure that the words that come out of your mouth (or that you type in an email message) are in harmony with the message you want to convey and the seriousness of the subject at hand.

Lincoln was a master at congruency. He knew when to apply a light touch and when to bear down with a firm hand. He resisted the urge to candy-coat the truth; if the situation was bad—as it was with Major General Hunter—he had the courage to say so, regardless of how uncomfortable the truth might be.

The president's capacity for unvarnished truth telling is evident in this 1862 letter to General McClellan, when he once again was forced to deal with a surly officer.

LETTER TO
GENERAL GEORGE MCCLELLAN
(APRIL 9, 1862)

My dear sir,

Your despatches, complaining that you are not properly sustained, while they do not offend me, do pain me very much. Blenker's division was withdrawn from you before you left here, and you knew the pressure under which I did it, and, as I thought, acquiesced in it certainly not without reluctance.

After you left I ascertained that less than 20,000 unorganized men, without a single field battery, were all you designed to be left for the defense of Washington and Manassas Junction, and part of this even to go to General Hooker's old position; General Banks's corps, once designed for Manassas Junction, was divided and tied up on the line of Winchester and Strasburg, and could not leave it without again exposing the upper Potomac and the Baltimore and Ohio Railroad. This presented (or would present when McDowell and Sumner should be gone) a great temptation to the enemy to turn back from the Rappahannock and sack Washington. My explicit order that Washington should, by the judgment of all the commanders of Army corps, be left entirely secure, had been neglected. It was precisely this that drove me to detain McDowell.

I do not forget that I was satisfied with your arrangement to leave Banks at Manassas Junction; but when that arrangement was broken up and nothing substituted for it, of course I was not satisfied. I was constrained to substitute something for it myself...

...And once more let me tell you it is indispensable to you that you strike a blow. I am powerless to help this. You will do me the justice to remember I always insisted that going down the bay in search of a field, instead of fighting at or near Manassas, was only shifting and not surmounting a

difficulty; that we would find the same enemy and the same or equal entrenchments at either place. The country will not fail to note—is noting now—that the present hesitation to move upon an entrenched enemy is but the story of Manassas repeated. I beg to assure you that I have never written you or spoken to you in greater kindness of feeling than now, nor with a fuller purpose to sustain you, so far as in my most anxious judgment I consistently can; but you must act.

Yours very truly,

A. Lincoln

In addition to breaking the bad news to his officers and encouraging them to keep doing their job despite their troubles, Lincoln was also quite adept at mixing the sweet with the sour. In the classic example on the next page—which should be required reading for the CEOs of every major *Fortune* 500 company—the president, in a few short paragraphs, gives one of his officers a huge promotion and also lets him know that he still has some work to do:

LETTER TO
MAJOR GENERAL HOOKER
(JANUARY 26, 1863)

General,

I have placed you at the head of the Army of the Potomac. Of course I have done this upon what appear to me to be sufficient reasons. And yet I think it best for you to know that there are some things in regard to which, I am not quite satisfied with you.

I believe you to be a brave and a skilful soldier, which, of course, I like. I also believe you do not mix politics with your profession, in which you are right. You have confidence in yourself, which is a valuable, if not an indispensable quality. You are ambitious, which, within reasonable bounds, does good rather than harm. But I think that during Gen. Burnside's command of the Army, you have taken counsel of your ambition, and thwarted him as much as you could, in which you did a great wrong to the country, and to a most meritorious and honorable brother officer.

I have heard, in such way as to believe it, of your recently saying that both the Army and the Government needed a Dictator. Of course it was not for this, but in spite of it, that

I have given you the command. Only those generals who gain successes, can set up dictators. What I now ask of you is military success, and I will risk the dictatorship.

The government will support you to the utmost of it's ability, which is neither more nor less than it has done and will do for all commanders. I much fear that the spirit which you have aided to infuse into the Army, of criticising their Commander, and withholding confidence from him, will now turn upon you. I shall assist you as far as I can, to put it down. Neither you, nor Napoleon, if he were alive again, could get any good out of an army, while such a spirit prevails in it.

And now, beware of rashness. Beware of rashness, but with energy, and sleepless vigilance, go forward, and give us victories.

Yours very truly,

A. Lincoln

Pay close attention to the structure of Lincoln's letter. In the first paragraph, Lincoln wove together the positive (Major General Hooker is being promoted) with the negative ("I am not quite satisfied with you"). It's a masterfully constructed opening meant to temper

Hooker's excitement with a cold dose of reality—and strongly implies that as quickly as the promotion was given, it could be taken away, unless Hooker addressed the shortcomings Lincoln outlined.

Lincoln continued this ping-ponging pattern. After ending on a rather sour note, he switched back to the positive in the second paragraph, listing Hooker's good qualities before zeroing in on a serious short-coming (thwarting General Burnside). He then went on to chastise Hooker for certain indiscreet political statements before warning him that the insolent behavior he showed toward Burnside may come back to haunt him: "I much fear that the spirit which you have aided to infuse into the Army, of criticising their Commander, and withholding confidence from him, will now turn upon you."

Why the negativity? After all, one could argue that Lincoln should be encouraging his new military leader, not filling his head with possible problems. But Lincoln wasn't trying to sabotage Hooker or undermine him before he even started the job. Just the opposite; he knew that in order for him to succeed, the major general had to be made aware of the pitfalls that awaited him—pitfalls of his own making.

The frankness with which Lincoln addressed Hooker also drives home the gravity of the situation. No doubt Hooker felt concerned, even worried after finishing Lincoln's letter…which was exactly the point. Lincoln was scaring him for all the right reasons: not because he desired a negative outcome, but because Hooker, for all of his skill as a military strategist, had not yet come to terms with his own fatal flaws.

Each time an employee is given a promotion or asked to tackle a new responsibility, he or she should be made aware of their supervisor's thoughts about their abilities. They deserve a frank assessment from their boss. Lincoln understood that.

CHAPTER 16

Encouraging Employees and Keeping up Morale

A S THE CIVIL WAR GOT UNDERWAY, ON TOP OF all his other worries Lincoln had to spearhead a massive logistical operation: troops needed to be mustered, supplies had to get from point A to point B, and a thousand other details demanded his immediate attention. Everyone was under a terrible strain. In those dark days, Lincoln knew that he had to do his best to keep up the troops' morale. In the two brief examples that follow, we find the sixteenth president of the United States at his best: encouraging, forthright, and unswervingly loyal.

Letter to Captain G.V. Fox, Washington D.C. (May 1, 1861)

My Dear Sir:

I sincerely regret that the failure of the late attempt to provision Fort Sumter should be the source of any annoyance to you.

The practicability of your plan was not, in fact, brought to a test. By reason of a gale, well known in advance to be possible and not improbable, the tugs, an essential part of the plan, never reached the ground; while, by an accident for which you were in no wise responsible, and possibly I to some extent was, you were deprived of a war vessel, with her men, which you deemed of great importance to the enterprise.

I most cheerfully and truly declare that the failure of the undertaking has not lowered you a particle, while the qualities you developed in the effort have greatly heightened you in my estimation.

For a daring and dangerous enterprise of a similar character you would to-day be the man of all my acquaintances whom I would select. You and I both anticipated that the cause of the country would be advanced by making the attempt to provision Fort Sumter, even if it should fail; and it is no small consolation now to feel that our anticipation is justified by the result.

Very truly your friend,

A. LINCOLN.

LETTER TO GENERAL GRANT
(APRIL 30, 1864)

Not expecting to see you again before the spring campaign opens, I wish to express in this way my entire satisfaction with what you have done up to this time, so far as I understand it.

The particulars of your plans I neither know nor seek to know. You are vigilant and self-reliant; and, pleased with this, I wish not to obtrude any constraints nor restraints upon you. While I am very anxious that any great disaster or capture of our men in great numbers shall be avoided, I know these points are less likely to escape your attention than they would be mine. If there is anything wanting which is within my power to give, do not fail to let me know it. And now, with a brave army and a just cause, may God sustain you.

Do your employees know how much you believe in them? How long has it been since you've encouraged them? Take a few minutes and write down the qualities that you admire in each of your subordinates, and when the time is right, let them in on the secret—you won't be disappointed in the results.

About the Author

David Acord has been a professional journalist and editor for more than twelve years. He is currently editor-in-chief of a business publishing company in Washington D.C. He received a bachelor of fine arts degree from Arkansas Tech University and a master of fine arts degree from the writing program at Penn State. He has been a Lincoln buff for most of his adult life and lives in Arlington, VA.